First World War
and Army of Occupation
War Diary
France, Belgium and Germany

38 DIVISION
Divisional Troops
Divisional Ammunition Column
19 December 1915 - 27 May 1919

WO95/2546/5

The Naval & Military Press Ltd
www.nmarchive.com
Published in association with The National Archives

Published by

The Naval & Military Press Ltd

Unit 10 Ridgewood Industrial Park,

Uckfield, East Sussex,

TN22 5QE England

Tel: +44 (0) 1825 749494

www.naval-military-press.com

www.nmarchive.com

This diary has been reprinted in facsimile from the original. Any imperfections are inevitably reproduced and the quality may fall short of modern type and cartographic standards.

© Crown Copyright
Images reproduced by permission of The National Archives, London, England, 2015.

Contents

Document type	Place/Title	Date From	Date To
Heading	WO95/2546/5		
Heading	38th Division Divl Artillery 38th Divl Ammn Column 1915 Dec-May 1919		
Heading	38th Div 38th D.A.C. Vol I Jan.16 May.19		
War Diary	Hazeley Down Winchester	19/12/1915	24/12/1915
War Diary	Havre	25/12/1915	26/12/1915
War Diary	Haverskerque	27/12/1915	31/12/1915
Heading	38th D.A.C. Vol 2		
War Diary	Haverskerque	03/01/1916	03/01/1916
War Diary	Paradis	31/01/1916	31/01/1916
Heading	38th D.A.C. Vol: 3		
War Diary	Paradis	04/02/1916	20/02/1916
Heading	38 Div AC. Vol 4		
War Diary	Mt. Bernenchon	04/03/1916	04/03/1916
War Diary	Mt. Bernenchon	03/03/1916	01/04/1916
War Diary	Robermetz De Merville	17/04/1916	28/05/1916
War Diary	Pont Riquel	29/05/1916	31/05/1916
Miscellaneous	XI Corps Q.M.5 First Army O.2.11/292 Q.M.G. Q.O.S/203/7/A. Appendix I	19/05/1916	19/05/1916
Miscellaneous	G.H.Q., O.B/818. Appendix I	14/05/1916	14/05/1916
Miscellaneous	Divisional Ammunition Column War Establishment.		
Miscellaneous	Divisional Ammunition Column War Establishment."A" Echelon.		
Miscellaneous	Divisional Ammunition Column War Establishment. "B" Echelon.		
Miscellaneous	Divisional Ammunition Column. War Establishment. (ii) Transport.		
Miscellaneous	Divisional Ammunition Column. War Establishment. (ii) Transport		
Miscellaneous	Statement Shewing Number Of Rounds Carried.		
Miscellaneous	Under the present system, the following personnel and vehicles are employed in a Division for Ammunition Supply Figures approximate only.		
Miscellaneous	O.C. D.A.C. Appendix 2	15/05/1916	15/05/1916
Miscellaneous	O.C. Appendix 3	15/05/1916	15/05/1916
Miscellaneous	Orders by Lt: Col. GW Hayward R.F.A. Commdg: 38th Dvl. Ammn Column Appendix 4	26/05/1916	26/05/1916
War Diary	Boisbergues	28/06/1916	28/06/1916
War Diary	Mirvaux	01/07/1916	01/07/1916
War Diary	Thiennes	12/06/1916	13/06/1916
War Diary	Auchel	15/06/1916	15/06/1916
War Diary	St. Michel	16/06/1916	22/06/1916
Operation(al) Order(s)	Operation Order No. 1. By Lt. Col. G.W. Hayward R.F.A. Comdg. 38th Div. Ammn. Column. Appendix 8	14/06/1916	14/06/1916
Map	Map Showing Distribution On Arrival.		
Miscellaneous	March Table		
Miscellaneous	March Table (38th Welsh Div. Order No. 30)		
Operation(al) Order(s)	38th (Welsh) Division Order No. 30 Appendix 9	12/06/1916	12/06/1916
Operation(al) Order(s)	Operation Order No 2 By Lt. Col. G.W. Hayward R.F.A. Comdg. 38th Div. Ammn Col. Appendix 10	15/06/1916	15/06/1916

Miscellaneous	Special Order Of The Day. By Major General Ivor Philipps. D.S.O. Commanding 38th (Welsh) Division. Appendix 11	14/06/1916	14/06/1916
Diagram etc	58th Division Camp and Watering Arrangements		
Miscellaneous	March Table (38th Divisional Artillery Order No. 17)		
Operation(al) Order(s)	38th Divisional Artillery. Operation Order No. 16. Appendix 5	10/06/1916	10/06/1916
Miscellaneous	R.A. 38th Div. No. G.S. 346. Appendix 6	11/06/1916	11/06/1916
Operation(al) Order(s)	38th Divisional Artillery Order No. 17. Appendix 7	12/06/1916	12/06/1916
Miscellaneous	Table "A"		
Heading	38th Div. XV. Corps. War Diary 38th Divisional Ammunition Column. July 1916		
War Diary	Toutencourt	02/07/1916	02/07/1916
War Diary	Treux	04/07/1916	05/07/1916
War Diary	Meaulte	06/07/1916	18/07/1916
War Diary	St. Leger	20/07/1916	20/07/1916
War Diary	Coigneux	21/07/1916	31/07/1916
Miscellaneous	Appendices 12 13 14 15 16 17 18 19		
Miscellaneous	A Form. Messages And Signals. Appendix 12		
Miscellaneous	Starting Point Fine of passing starting point.		
Miscellaneous	A Form. Messages And Signals. Appendix 13		
Miscellaneous	March Table		
Miscellaneous	A Form. Messages And Signals. Appendix 14	06/07/1916	06/07/1916
Miscellaneous	All Services. Appendix 15	13/07/1916	13/07/1916
Operation(al) Order(s)	38th D.A.C. Order No 7. Appendix 16	14/07/1916	14/07/1916
Operation(al) Order(s)	38th Divisional Artillery Order No. 24 Appx 17	19/07/1916	19/07/1916
Miscellaneous	March Table		
Miscellaneous	38th. D.A.C. Order No. 10. Appendix 18	29/07/1916	29/07/1916
Operation(al) Order(s)	Addenda to 38th D.A.C. Order No 10	29/07/1916	29/07/1916
Miscellaneous	S.A.A. Section 38 D.A.C. Composition of Trains.		
Miscellaneous	Fourth Army. Appendix 19	18/07/1916	18/07/1916
Miscellaneous	O.C. D.A.C.	21/07/1916	21/07/1916
War Diary	Thievres	07/08/1916	08/08/1916
War Diary	Bretel	10/08/1916	10/08/1916
War Diary	Rubrouck	14/08/1916	15/08/1916
War Diary	Nr. Peselhoek A21a8.3 (Sheet 28).	23/08/1916	24/08/1916
War Diary	Nr. Peselhoek	29/08/1916	31/08/1916
Operation(al) Order(s)	38th Divisional Artillery Order No. 28 Appedix 20	05/08/1916	05/08/1916
Miscellaneous	Table Of Relief In Action		
Miscellaneous	Relief Of Wagon Lines		
Miscellaneous	O.C. D.A.C. Appx.21	05/08/1916	05/08/1916
Miscellaneous	Wagon Lines. R.A. Headquarters-Bus. 119th. Brigade R.F.A.		
Operation(al) Order(s)	38th D.A.C. Order No. 11. Appx 22	06/08/1916	06/08/1916
Operation(al) Order(s)	38th Divisional Artillery Order No. 29 Appx 23	09/08/1916	09/08/1916
Miscellaneous	March Table		
Operation(al) Order(s)	38th D.A.C.-Order No. 12 Appx 24	09/08/1916	09/08/1916
Miscellaneous	R.A. 38th Div. No. G.S.671	11/08/1916	11/08/1916
Operation(al) Order(s)	38th Divisional Artillery Order No. 30. Appx 25	11/08/1916	11/08/1916
Miscellaneous	Strategical Move Of 38th (Welsh) Divisional Artillery.	07/08/1916	07/08/1916
Miscellaneous	Table "D" 38th (Welsh) Divisional Artillery.		
Miscellaneous	Order No 13	12/08/1916	12/08/1916
Operation(al) Order(s)	38th D.A.C. Order No. 13. By Lt. Col. GW Hayward R.F.A. Commdg 38 DAC Appx 26	13/08/1916	13/08/1916
Operation(al) Order(s)	38th Divisional Artillery Order No. 31. Appx 27	19/08/1916	19/08/1916
Miscellaneous	Table Of Reliefs		

Type	Description	Date From	Date To
Miscellaneous	R.A. 38th Div. No. B.K.25	19/08/1916	19/08/1916
Miscellaneous	R.A. 38th Div. No. G.S.715	19/08/1916	19/08/1916
Miscellaneous	38th. Divisional Artillery. Relief Of Wagon Lines and D.A.C. Appx 28	22/08/1916	22/08/1916
Miscellaneous			
Operation(al) Order(s)	38th D.A.C. Order No. 12. Appx 29	23/08/1916	23/08/1916
War Diary	Peselhoek	04/09/1916	26/11/1916
War Diary	Herzeele	15/12/1916	31/12/1916
Operation(al) Order(s)	38th D.A.C. Order No. 19. Appendix 31	14/12/1916	14/12/1916
Operation(al) Order(s)	Amendment To 38th D.A.C. Order No: 19	14/12/1916	14/12/1916
Operation(al) Order(s)	38th Divisional Artillery Order No. 41 Appendix 30	12/12/1916	12/12/1916
Miscellaneous	Appendix		
Operation(al) Order(s)	38th Divisional Artillery Order No. 42	12/12/1916	12/12/1916
Operation(al) Order(s)	Corrections To 38th Divisional Artillery Orders Nos. 41 And 42	12/12/1916	12/12/1916
War Diary	Herzeele	13/01/1917	13/01/1917
War Diary	Peselhoek	18/01/1917	27/01/1917
Operation(al) Order(s)	38th Divisional Artillery Order No. 46 Appendix 32	13/01/1917	13/01/1917
Miscellaneous	To Accompany 38th Divisional Artillery Order No. 46 Appendix "A"		
Operation(al) Order(s)	Appendix "B" To Accompany 38th Divisional Artillery Order No. 46		
Miscellaneous	O.C. DAC	14/01/1917	14/01/1917
Miscellaneous	List of Area Stores Which are to be Handed Over to Relieving Units.		
Operation(al) Order(s)	Amendment To 38th Divisional Order No. 46		
Operation(al) Order(s)	38th D.A.C. Order No:20. Appendix 33	16/01/1917	16/01/1917
War Diary	Peselhoek	03/02/1917	30/05/1917
Operation(al) Order(s)	38th. Divisional Artillery Operation Order No. 63. Appx 36	16/05/1917	16/05/1917
Miscellaneous	Table Of Reliefs		
Operation(al) Order(s)	Administrative Instructions To Accompany R.A. Operation Order No. 63	16/05/1917	16/05/1917
Operation(al) Order(s)	38th Divisional Ammunition Column. Order No. 22	17/05/1917	17/05/1917
Operation(al) Order(s)	38th. Divisional Artillery Operation Order No. 62. Appendix 35	02/05/1917	02/05/1917
Miscellaneous	Appendix "A".		
Operation(al) Order(s)	Administrative Instructions To Accompany R.A. Order No. 62	02/05/1917	02/05/1917
Operation(al) Order(s)	Amendment To 38th Divisional Artillery Operation Order No. 62	05/05/1917	05/05/1917
Operation(al) Order(s)	Amendment To Administrative Instructions To Accompany R.A. Order No. 62	02/05/1917	02/05/1917
War Diary	Peselhoek	03/06/1917	03/06/1917
War Diary	Coppernolle	06/06/1917	15/09/1917
War Diary	Steenvoorde	16/09/1917	16/09/1917
War Diary	La Cunewele	17/09/1917	17/09/1917
War Diary	Steenbecque	19/09/1917	21/09/1917
War Diary	Estaires	21/09/1917	26/01/1918
War Diary	Haverskerque	06/02/1918	17/02/1918
War Diary	Steenwerk	01/03/1918	30/03/1918
Heading	V. Corps. Third Army. War Diary 38th Divisional Ammunition Column. April 1918		
War Diary	Steenwerk	07/04/1918	07/04/1918
War Diary	Haverskerque	08/04/1918	08/04/1918
War Diary	Neuf Berquin	08/04/1918	08/04/1918

War Diary	La Motte	11/04/1918	11/04/1918
War Diary	Gd Sec Bois	12/04/1918	12/04/1918
War Diary	Borre	12/04/1918	12/04/1918
War Diary	Morbecque	20/04/1918	20/04/1918
War Diary	Bois des Huit Rues	21/04/1918	24/04/1918
War Diary	Morbecque Bois des Huit Rues	07/05/1918	08/05/1918
War Diary	St Jan Ter Biezen	13/05/1918	18/05/1918
War Diary	Gezaincourt.	21/05/1918	31/05/1918
War Diary	Raincheval	10/06/1918	24/08/1918
War Diary	Hedauville	24/08/1918	24/08/1918
War Diary	Albert	25/08/1918	25/08/1918
War Diary	Contalmaison	27/08/1918	28/08/1918
War Diary	Mametz Wood	29/08/1918	29/08/1918
War Diary	Trones Wood	02/09/1918	03/09/1918
War Diary	Le Sars	07/09/1918	07/09/1918
War Diary	Bus	10/09/1918	10/09/1918
War Diary	Vallulart Wood	12/09/1918	01/10/1918
War Diary	Dessart Wood	05/10/1918	05/10/1918
War Diary	Catalet Valley	06/10/1918	06/10/1918
War Diary	Ossus Wood	08/10/1918	08/10/1918
War Diary	Honnecourt.	09/10/1918	10/10/1918
War Diary	Clary	14/10/1918	15/10/1918
War Diary	Bertry	24/10/1918	24/10/1918
War Diary	Bertry	18/10/1918	18/10/1918
War Diary	Bertry	08/10/1918	08/10/1918
War Diary	Bertry	01/10/1918	01/10/1918
War Diary	Montay	05/11/1918	05/11/1918
War Diary	Wagonville	06/11/1918	06/11/1918
War Diary	Grande Pature	14/11/1918	14/11/1918
War Diary	Aulnoye	28/12/1918	28/12/1918
War Diary	Montay	29/12/1918	29/12/1918
War Diary	Masnieres	30/12/1918	30/12/1918
War Diary	Manancourt	31/12/1918	31/12/1918
War Diary	Aulnoye	28/12/1918	28/12/1918
War Diary	Montay	29/12/1918	29/12/1918
War Diary	Masnieres	30/12/1918	30/12/1918
War Diary	Manancourt	31/12/1918	31/12/1918
War Diary	Albert.	01/01/1919	01/01/1919
War Diary	Montigny	22/01/1919	23/01/1919
War Diary	Glisy	10/04/1919	27/05/1919

HO/S / 2546 / 6.

38TH DIVISION
DIVL ARTILLERY

38TH DIVL AMMN COLUMN
1915 DEC ~~JAN 1916~~ - MAY 1919

38th ẔŪ 1

38èt S.A.C.
Vol. I

121/7824

Jan. 16
May 19

Army Form C. 2118

WAR DIARY
or
INTELLIGENCE SUMMARY

(Erase heading not required.)

38th Divisional Ammⁿ. Column
W.A.C.

Instructions regarding War Diaries and Intelligence Summaries are contained in F.S. Regs., Part II. and the Staff Manual respectively. Title Pages will be prepared in manuscript.

Place	Date	Hour	Summary of Events and Information	Remarks and references to Appendices
HAZELEY DOWN. WINCHESTER	19/12/15	10 p.m.	Orders received that 38th Div Arty. will embark on 22nd, & 23rd. December, 1915.	
—	23/12/15	10 p.m.	No. 3 Section (3 Officers, 143 Other Ranks, 221 animals, 33 Vehicles) under command of Capt. J. PLUMMER left WINCHESTER at 8 a.m. and proceeded by march route to SOUTHAMPTON. This section embarked on S.S. BELLEROPHON together with Brigade Ammunition Columns of 121st. and 122nd Brigades, R.F.A. The vessel sailed at 5.30 p.m. and the section was disembarked at HAVRE at 10 a.m. 24/12/15. Casualties nil.	
—	24/12/15	10 p.m.	The remainder of the Column left WINCHESTER in the following order, by route march for SOUTHAMPTON. D & E Subsections under LIEUT. J.H. PALMER at 4.30 a.m. A & B Subsections under LIEUT. S.H. HILDYARD at 6 a.m. C & F Subsections and Head Quarters under Lt. Col. G.W. HAYWARD at 8 a.m. The whole of the above embarked on S.S. NIRVANA and sailed at 5 p.m. A very rough crossing was experienced. 1 horse and 6 mules died and 13 Wagons were so much damaged that they had to be exchanged for new. Arrived off HAVRE at 3 a.m. 25/12/15 and disembarked at 11 am. Disembarking took 4 hours owing to state of Wagons and condition of animals after the voyage. No.3. Quartermaster Ray train at 8 p.m. No. 2 Section (less E Subsection) left by train at 8 p.m. (less F Subsection)	
HAVRE	25/12/15	10 p.m.	E & F Subsections entrained at 8 a.m. C Subsection & Head Quarters entrained at 10 a.m.	
—	26/12/15	10 p.m.	No. 1 Section (less C Subsection entrained at 8 p.m.	

Army Form C. 2118

WAR DIARY
or
INTELLIGENCE SUMMARY
(Erase heading not required.)

Instructions regarding War Diaries and Intelligence Summaries are contained in F.S. Regs., Part II. and the Staff Manual respectively. Title Pages will be prepared in manuscript.

Place	Date	Hour	Summary of Events and Information	Remarks and references to Appendices
HAVERSKERQUE	27/12/15	10 p.m.	G and H Subsections detrained at MERVILLE at 10 p.m. 26/12/15 & marched to this place. D and F Subsections detrained at LESTREM at about 1 p.m. and marched to this place. E and I Subsections detrained at MERVILLE at 10.30 a.m. and marched to this place. C Subsection and Head Quarters detrained at MERVILLE at 12 noon and marched to this place.	
" "	28/12/15	10 p.m.	A & B Subsections detrained at LESTREM at 12.45 a.m. and marched to this place. The whole unit is now concentrated. Head Quarters are billeted in HAVERSKERQUE. Nos. 1 & 3 Section about half mile NORTH. No 2 Section at LE FORÊT.	
" "	31/12/15	10 p.m.	The whole column have been engaged since arrival in smartening up the wagons hoods and improving billets and horse lines. Officers present:— Lt. Col. G.W. HAYWARD (Commanding) Capt. C.W.E. ALLEN. (Adjutant) LIEUT. W. HERBERTSON. (Medical Officer) LIEUT. S.H. HILDYARD (Comdg No 1 Section) LIEUT. T. HAYES-SHEEN 2/LIEUT. K.K. HUGHES	

WAR DIARY

INTELLIGENCE SUMMARY

Army Form C. 2118

Place	Date	Hour	Summary of Events and Information	Remarks and references to Appendices
HAVERSKERQUE	31/12/15	10pm	LIEUT. J.H. PALMER (Comdg. No.2 Section) LIEUT. M.H. BERNSTEIN 2/LIEUT. A.A. MORRIS CAPT. J. PLUMMER (Comdg. No.3 Section) 2/LIEUT. J.H. LLEWELLYN 2/LIEUT. L. HORWOOD Warrant Officers. 27407 A/R.S.M. W.J. PYE 62786 B.S.M. A. KENTFIELD 82950 B.S.M. W.T. LEWIS 31328 B.S.M. J. WILLIAMS 57589 B.Q.M.S. W.J. TUBBY Other ranks 543. Animals 67. Wagons G.S. 96. Water Carts 2. Maltese Cart 1. Bicycles 5. E.H. Hayward Lt. Col. R.A. Comdg. 38th Div. Ammn. Column	

38½ bl. skr.
fol 2

Army Form C. 2118

WAR DIARY
INTELLIGENCE SUMMARY

38th. D.A.C.

(Erase heading not required.)

Instructions regarding War Diaries and Intelligence Summaries are contained in F. S. Regs., Part II. and the Staff Manual respectively. Title Pages will be prepared in manuscript.

Place	Date	Hour	Summary of Events and Information	Remarks and references to Appendices
HAVERSKERQUE	3/1/16	10 pm	Orders received to-day that Establishments of S.A.A. & Howitzer ammunition whole in future be:- S.A.A. 586,000 rounds & 404 Howitzer rounds as against previous establishment of S.A.A. 930,000 rounds & 468 Howitzer.	
PARADIS	31/1/16	10 pm	The Column moved up to relieve the 19th. D.A.C. to-day. Headquarters & Reserve in PARADIS. No. 1 Section at PACAUT. No. 2 Section at CORNET MALO and No. 3 Section at BOUZATEUX FARM. The four wagons per section, carrying Howitzer ammunition, have been withdrawn and formed into a separate section under the command of LIEUT. T. HAYES-SHEEN. It is thought that this arrangement will conduce to efficiency and smooth running. Notes will be made from time to time as to the efficacy of this arrangement.	31/1/16

E.G. Hayward
Lt. Col. R.A.
Comdg. 38th Divisional Ammunition Column

38th D.A.E.
Vol: 3

Army Form C. 2118

WAR DIARY
or
INTELLIGENCE SUMMARY
(Erase heading not required.)

Instructions regarding War Diaries and Intelligence Summaries are contained in F. S. Regs., Part II. and the Staff Manual respectively. Title Pages will be prepared in manuscript.

Place	Date	Hour	Summary of Events and Information	Remarks and references to Appendices
PARADIS	4/2/16	10 pm	2nd Lieuts. A. F. SHERT and C. THOMAS joined today from England.	
	10/2/16	10 pm	REV. R. O. LLOYD. C.F. joined today from England.	
	13/2/16	10 pm	13 H Driver E. L. James sent one hour wounded by shrapnel. He was on fatigue in LA COUTURE.	
	19/2/16	10 pm	6628 Gnr. C. DENTON attached 67 T.M. Battery wounded — Shell shock.	
	20/2/16	10 pm	6285 Gnr. A. WALMSLEY attached 67 T.M. Battery wounded — Shell shock.	

Lt. Col. R.A.
Comdg. 38 K. Div. Ammn. Col.

29/2/16

38

38 DwAC
Vol 4

Army Form C. 2118

WAR DIARY
INTELLIGENCE SUMMARY
(Erase heading not required.)

Instructions regarding War Diaries and Intelligence Summaries are contained in F. S. Regs., Part II. and the Staff Manual respectively. Title Pages will be prepared in manuscript.

Place	Date	Hour	Summary of Events and Information	Remarks and references to Appendices
MT. BERNENCHON	9/3/16	10 pm	The Column marched from PARADIS Kortery.	
	3/7/16		Rev R.O. LLOYD, C.F. posten to 114th. Infantry Brigade.	
	26/7/16	11pm	20 men posted to TRENCH MORTAR SCHOOL ST. VENANT & from 238 Trench mortar Battery.	

W. Wyllie Capt. R.E.
Comdy. 38th. D.A.C.

Vol 2

Army Form C. 2118

WAR DIARY
or
INTELLIGENCE SUMMARY
(Erase heading not required.)

38th. Divl. Amb. Coy. (W.A.C.)

Instructions regarding War Diaries and Intelligence Summaries are contained in F. S. Regs., Part II. and the Staff Manual respectively. Title Pages will be prepared in manuscript.

Place	Date	Hour	Summary of Events and Information	Remarks and references to Appendices
MT BERNENCHON	1/4/16		We have, today, sent away to G.S. Wagons and in future be kept by three wagons and 24 animals. The animals will be absorbed in replacement of casualties.	
ROBERMETZ DE MERVILLE	17/4/16	10pm	The Column moved here today in relief of 19th. D.A.C.	

E.D. Hayward
Lt. Col. R.A.
Comdg. 38th. D.A.C. (W.A.C.)

1875 Wt. W593/826 1,000,000 4/15 J.B.C. & A. A.D.S.S./Forms/C. 2118.

WAR DIARY
INTELLIGENCE SUMMARY
(Erase heading not required.)

Army Form C. 2118

38th Div. Ammn. Col. (W.A.C.) Vol 6

Place	Date	Hour	Summary of Events and Information	Remarks and references to Appendices
ROBERMETZ DE MERVILLE	13/5/16		2/Lieut. C. THOMAS posted to 119th Brigade R.F.A.	
	15/9/16		Orders received to commence re-organisation of D.A.C. The unit in its arriving of 4 sections, 1, 2 & 3 sections being known as 'A' echelon and 4th section as 'B' Echelon. Composition to be as shown in appendix I. The first step towards this is the forming of 'B' Echelon. Capt. Parry has joined and orders have been issued for the forming of Ammunition Columns (appendix 2)	G.H.Q.O.B/3/818. Appendix 1 attached. 38 Div Arty TA/999 appendix 2
	16/5/16		The formation of 'B' Echelon has been completed as far as is possible from the existing D.A.C.	
	17/5/16		The three sections of 'A' echelon have now been organised in readiness to receive the personnel, animals and vehicles to complete them to their new establishment. A camp has been established for the reception of all surplus personnel, animals and vehicles.	
	18/5/16		To-day the personnel, animals and vehicles shown in appendix 3 have been and have been allotted to sections of 'A' echelon, and have taken over their duties with regard to ammunition supply. The officers who have joined are Lieuts. P.R. DANGERFIELD., A. WYNNE-WILLIAMS and T.J. JONES.	38 Div Arty TA/999 Appendix 3.

WAR DIARY or INTELLIGENCE SUMMARY

Army Form C. 2118

(Erase heading not required) 381k.

Place	Date	Hour	Summary of Events and Information	Remarks and references to Appendices
ROBERMETZ DE MERVILLE	19/5/16		Further work done today in arranging sections and "weeding out" personnel and animals for evacuation.	
	24/5/16		The remaining details, personnel, animals and vehicles of Res Ammn Col. formed today the section of "A" Echelon now complete and moved up to the position previously occupied by Res Ammn Column at PONT RIQUEL. Major B.P. Burroughs has been placed in command of Supplies Details which are being formed into two sections under the command of Lieut. J.S. Arnold and Lieut. G. Copp. The following officers joined to-day. Major B.P. BURROUGHS Lieut. J.E. RANSLEY " R.K. GREEN " J.S. ARNOLD 2/Lieut. F.L. HYBART " G. COPP	
	25/5/16		Lieut. M.H. BERNSTEIN posted to TRENCH MORTAR Battery.	
	26/5/16		Lieut. A.F. SHORT posted to 128th Brigade R.F.A.	
	28/5/16		Lieut. T. DAWKING-WILLIAMS joined from 120th Brigade R.F.A. 2/Lieut. L. HORWOOD posted to 128th Brigade R.F.A.	

Army Form C. 2118

WAR DIARY
or
INTELLIGENCE SUMMARY

38th Div Ammn Col (WAC)

(Erase heading not required.)

Place	Date	Hour	Summary of Events and Information	Remarks and references to Appendices
ROBERMETZ DE MERVILLE	28/5/16		The supplies details left today by march route to CALAIS. (Appendix 4) There now remain 11 Wagons G.S. and a quantity of harness to be sent by rail.	Appendix 4 to be sent by rail attached
PONT RIQUEL	29/5/16		Headquarters moved today to PONT RIQUEL.	
"	30/5/16		Major B.P. Burroughs, Capt. J.H. Palmer and Lieut. J.S. Arnold rejoined.	
"	31/5/16		Capt. J.H. Palmer posted for duty with Reserve details CALAIS. "A" Echelon is now situated at PONT RIQUEL and "B" Echelon at ROBERMETZ DE MERVILLE.	

31/5/16

[signed]
Lt. Col R.E.
Comdg 38th Divl Ammn Column

XI Corps Q.M.5

First Army O.S.11/292
Q..G. Q.O.S/203/7/A.

First Army

With reference to letter No.O.B./818 dated 6th instant giving the reorganization of the Divisional Artillery, the following action should be taken in regard to the equipment and spares on charge of Divisional Artillery units, pending the publication of new Mob: Store Tables.

O.B/818
Para.(a)i

1. **Old Regular Divisions.**

The 4.5" Howitzer Batteries move to their Brigades intact, but the Headquarters of the Howitzer Brigades are to be withdrawn.
The equipment on charge of these Brigade Headquarters should be returned to the Base.

O.B/818
Para.(a)ii

2. **Other Divisions (T.F. & N.A.).**

The Headquarters of the Howitzer Brigades become the Headquarters of the 4th mixed Brigade.
The equipment at present authorised under the Mobilization Store Table for a 4.5" Howitzer Brigade Headquarters should be retained, and any extra equipment that may be allowed under the Mobilization Store Table for an 18-pdr Brigade H.Qrs and which is considered necessary, should be drawn under A.F. G.1098-106.
The Batteries of the Howitzer Brigade move intact to their new Brigades.

O.B/818
Para.(b)

3. **Divisional Ammunition Column.**

The Headquarters remains intact with the addition of one Maltese cart for Medical equipment and one water cart, the latter of which is available from the old Brigade Ammunition Column.

Echelon 'A'. The Brigade Ammunition Columns of the three 18-pr Brigades and of the 4.5" Howitzer Brigade come back intact, (except for the reduction of one water cart) and are complete with equipment and spares. They are to be re-adjusted to form the three mobile sections of Echelon 'A'.
One G.S. wagon for technical stores is allowed to each mobile section of echelon 'A', the fourth wagon being transferred to echelon 'B'.
The stores carried by these wagons should therefore be distributed to the best advantage between the four wagons.

Echelon 'B'. The re-organization entails the return of 44 G.S. wagons to the Base and they should be returned complete with their wagon equipment.
The spares, tools and materials authorised for a Divisional Ammunition Column should be retained and distributed amongst the various G.S. wagons of the Section.

- 2 -

Mobilization Store Tables.

Mobilization Store Tables are in process of being drawn up by the War Office, but in the meantime the following tables should be utilized :-

All Brigade Headquarters	A.F.G.1098-106.	
6-gun Batteries 18-pr. Old Divisions	do.	14.
O.B/818 4-gun Batteries 18-pr. Other Divisions	do.	106.
Para(a)ii 4-gun Batteries 4.5" How. All Divisions.	do.	263.
H.Q., Divisional Ammunition Column.	do.	10.
'A' Echelon - composed of :-		
3 18-pr. Bde.Ammn.Cols.	do.	106
1 4.5" How.Bde.Ammn.Col.	do.	263

'B' Echelon - as a temporary measure A.F.G.1098-108 should be utilized, the personal and wagon equipment being based on the personnel and vehicles authorised, while the spares, tools and materials to be carried will be as shown in A.F.G.1098-108.

G.H.Q.
17th May.1916.

(sd) A.Forbes, Colonel,
D.D.O.S.
for Quartermaster General.

Headquarters,
   33rd Division.
   35th Division.
   38th Division.
   39th Division.
   61st Division.

Forwarded in continuation of XI Corps R.H.S./859/4 dated 14.5.1916.

Please issue the necessary instructions to all concerned.

XI Corps.
19. 5. 16.

A.F.N.Green
Lieut Colonel,
A.Q.M.G., XI Corps.

HP

SECRET.   G.H.Q., O.B/818.   XIth Corps.
             First Army C/569 10/5/16.   RHS/859/4.
             D.D.S.T. No. C/277 10/5/16.

Subject :- Reorganisation of Divisional Artillery.

Headquarters,
   33rd Division.
   35th Division.
   38th Division.
   39th Division.

Appendix 1.

1.   In accordance with G.H.Q., OB/818 of 6th May, 1916, the Artillery of all Divisions of XIth Corps will be reorganised forthwith as under.

2.   **Formation of Mixed Brigades.**
       In all Divisions one howitzer battery will be substituted for one 18-pounder battery in each of the 18-pounder brigades.
       The three 18-pounder batteries thus displaced will form the fourth brigade under the former Howitzer Brigade Headquarters.
       The artillery of 33rd Division (with 12 howitzers) will then consist of three mixed brigades and one 18-pounder brigade constituted as follows :-

       Three mixed brigades........Three 18-pdr batteries and one howitzer battery.
       One 18-pounder brigade......Three 18-pdr batteries.

       The artillery of the 35th, 38th, and 39th Divisions (with 16 howitzers) will consist of four mixed brigades, each brigade containing three 18-pdr batteries and one howitzer battery.
       Changes in the nomenclature of batteries necessitated by transfers from one Brigade to another will be reported through the usual channel to General Headquarters showing in each case the old and the new designation.   The letter "D" will be assigned to the howitzer battery in each brigade.

3.   **Reorganisation of the System of Ammunition Supply within the Division.**
       (i).   The Brigade Ammunition Columns will be abolished as such.
       (ii). The Divisional Ammunition Column will be reconstituted in two echelons composed as follows :-

              Headquarters.
              A Echelon, consisting of Nos. 1, 2 and 3 Sections.
              B Echelon, consisting of No. 4 Section.

          Headquarters and A Echelon are designed to accompany the
              Divisions closely at all times.
          B Echelon will follow the Division if circumstances
              permit, but is detachable under Corps control when
              necessary.

4.   The following tables are attached :-

       (a). Divisional Ammunition Column, War Establishment.
       (b). Statement showing number of rounds carried.
       (c). Statement of personnel and vehicles employed in a Division for ammunition Supply.

5. In accordance with Q.M.G. letter Q.4961 of 6-5-16, the personnel, horses, harness and vehicles which become surplus on the reorganisation of the Divisional Ammunition Columns will be used to complete other establishments, and the surplus then remaining will be evacuated. This opportunity will be taken to exchange and evacuate all Mark IV G.S. Wagons still remaining in possession of Divisions.

Such surplus will be moved by march route to CALAIS and there demobilized under arrangements made by the I.G.C.

Surplus of 33rd Division to arrive at CALAIS on May 28th.
,, 35th ,, ,, ,, May 31st.
,, 38th ,, ,, ,, June 3rd.
,, 39th ,, ,, ,, June 5th.

Route and halting places will be notified later.

6. Divisional Commanders will notify Base Commandant, CALAIS, of :-

(i). Date of departure.
(ii). Date and probable hour of arrival.
(iii). Strength.

7. Rations and forage for the march and for the day following that of arrival will be taken in the wagons.

8. Any surplus vehicles which cannot be horsed will be despatched by rail to the Base.

9. Form A (attached) will be filled in by each Division and rendered to XIth Corps Headquarters as soon as exact figures are known.

10. Report early when you expect to have completed the reorganisation.

11. Instructions as to disposal of surplus ammunition will be issued later.

12. Acknowledge.

XIth Corps.
14th May, 1916.

sd/. W.H. ANDERSON,
B.G., G.S.

Copies to :-
A.D.O.S.
B.G., R.A.

DIVISIONAL AMMUNITION COLUMN

War Establishment. (continued)

Detail	Personnel								Horses					Bicycles	Motor Cycles
	Officers	Warrant Officers	Clerks	Staff Serjts & Serjeants	Artificers	Trumpeters	Rank and File	TOTAL	Riding	Draught	Heavy Draught	Pack	TOTAL		

COMPOSITION IN DETAIL.

Detail	Off	WO	Clk	SS	Art	Tr	R&F	Tot	Rid	Dr	HD	Pk	Tot	Bic	MC
Headquarters,-															
Lieutenant-Colonel	1							1	2				2		
Adjutant	1							1	2				2	1	
Serjeant-Major ...		1						1	1				1		
Artillery Clerk...			1					1	1				1		
Artillery Clerk...			1					1						1	
Battery Qr.Mr.Serjt				1				1	1				1		
Clerk							1	1						1	
Gunners... ...							1	1	1				1		
Orderlies for M.O.) (c))							3	3	4				4		
(for vehicles							10	10		20			20		
Drivers(for spare draught horses							2	2		4			4		
(spare ...							2	2							
Batmen (d) ...							5	5							
Total Headquarters (excluding attached)	2	1	2				24	29	7	28			35		
Attached -															
R.A.M.C. (includes personnel for water duties)	1						0e+3	4	1				1		
Serjeants, A.V.C. (f)				4				4	4				4		
Drivers, A.S.C. (train transport)							13	13			26		26		
Total Headquarters (including attached)	3	1	2	6			27	37	12	28			40		

(b). Attached to A.G's office at the Base.
(c). 8 men (1 an acting bombardier) trained to the duties are placed under the orders of the medical officer. The gunners drive the carts for medical equipment.
(d). All batmen are fully armed and trained soldiers, and are available for duty in the ranks.
(e). Includes a corporal.
(f). One per section.

DIVISIONAL AMMUNITION COLUMN

War Establishment. (continued).

'A' ECHELON.

Detail	Officers	Warrant Officers	Clerks	Staff Serjts & Serjeants	Artificers	Trumpeters	Rank and File	TOTAL	Riding	Draught	Heavy Draught	Pack	TOTAL	Bicycles	Motor Cycles
COMPOSITION IN DETAIL.															
Nos: 1, 2 & 3 Sections each -															
Captain	1							1	1				1		
Subalterns	2							2	2				2		
Battery Serjeant-Major		1						1	1				1		
Battery Qr.Mr.Serjeant			1					1	1				1		
Serjeants				4				4	4				4		
Farrier Serjeant					1			1	1				1		
Shoeing Smiths					5(e)			5	1				1		
Saddlers					2(h)			2							
Fitters or Wheelers					1			1							
Corporals							4	4	4				4		
Bombardiers							5	5	3				3		
Gunners							40	40	1				1		
Drivers (for vehicles							89	89		178			178		
Drivers (for spare draught horses							8	8		16			16		
Drivers (spare							4	4							
Batmen							3	3							
Total	3	1	5	9			153	171	19	194			213		

(e). Includes a corporal.

(h). 2 of the 6 saddlers and 1 of the 3 fitters or wheelers will be corporals.

NOTE :- The above establishment includes 7 acting bombardiers.

DIVISIONAL AMMUNITION COLUMN.

War Establishment. (continued).

'B' ECHELON.

Detail	Personnel								Horses					Bicycles	Motor Cars
	Officers	Warrant Officers	Clerks	Staff Serjeants & Serjeants	Artificers	Trumpeters	Rank & File	TOTAL	Riding	Draught	Heavy Draught	Pack	TOTAL		
COMPOSITION IN DETAIL.															
No: 4 Section -															
Captain	1							1	1				1		
Subalterns	3							3	3				3		
Battery Serjt.-Major		1						1	1				1		
Battery Qr.Mr.Serjt.				1				1	1				1		
Serjeants				6				6	6				6		
Farrier Serjeant					1			1	1						
Shoeing Smiths					7(e)			7	1				1		
Saddlers					3(e)			3							
Fitters or Wheelers					1			1							
Corporals							6	6	6				6		
Bombardiers							7	7	1				1		
Gunners							57	57							
Drivers (for vehicles							141	141		282			282		
(for spare draught horses							14	14		28			28		
(spare							7	7							
Batmen							4	4							
Total Section	4	1		7	12		236	260	21	310			331		

(e). Includes a corporal.

<u>NOTE</u> :- The above establishment includes 9 acting bombardiers.

DIVISIONAL AMMUNITION COLUMN.

War Establishment.

(ii) Transport.

Detail	Headquarters				1st, 2nd & 3-rd Sections				4th Section				TOTAL			
	Vehicles	Drivers	Draught Horses	Heavy Draught Horses	Vehicles	Drivers	Draught Horses	Heavy Draught Horses	Vehicles	Drivers	Draught Horses	Heavy Draught Horses	Vehicles	Drivers	Draught Horses	Heavy Draught Horses
Bicycles for intercommunication (j)	2	(k)2			9				3				14	(k)2		
Carts, maltese for medical equipment	2	2	4						1	1	2		3	3	6	
Carts, water	2	3	4		3	9	18		1	3	6		5	15	30	
Carts, technical stores	1	3	6										1	3	6	
Carts, explosives	1	3	6										2	4	8	
Wagons, cooks	1	2	4						1	2	4		2	4	8	
Wagons, G.S.					18	54	108		20	60	120		38	114	228	
Wagons for S.A.A.									12	36	72		12	36	72	
Wagons for 18-pounder									12	36	72		12	36	72	
Wagons for 4.5-inch									1	3	6		4	12	24	
Wagons for grenades					3	9	18						48	144	288	
Wagons, limbered (for 18-pdr with limbers)(for 4.5-in. limbered)					48	144	288						12	36	72	
Wagons, limbered G.S. for S.A.A.					12	36	72						15	15	30	
Drivers (for spare horses) (spare)		2	4		15	15	30			14	28			40	80	
		2				24	48			7				21		
						12										
Train. Wagons (supplies)(l) (for baggage and) (for extra forage)	1(m)	1(m)		2	6	(m)6		12	3(m)	3(m)		6	10(m)	10(m)		20
	2(m)	2(m)		4					1(m)	1(m)		2	3(m)	3(m)		6
Total	9	16	28		108	303	582		51	162	310		168	481	920	

(NOTES

DIVISIONAL AMMUNITION COLUMN.

War Establishment. (continued)

(ii) Transport (continued)

(j) Riders will be detailed as required from rank and file.
(k) Medical Officer's orderlies.
(l) Arrangements may, if necessary, be made for the carriage of the Headquarters' baggage in the baggage wagon or wagons of one or more sections.
(m) Provided from the Divisional Train.

NOTE :-

In Divisions having 16 Howitzers, the following will be added :-

'A' Echelon .... Wagons, Ammunition with limbers....4
                 Drivers 12
                 Horses 24

'B' Echelon .... G.S. Wagons 4
                 Drivers 12
                 Horses 24

(b).

STATEMENT SHOWING NUMBER OF ROUNDS CARRIED.

	With Batt.	"A" echelon.	"B" echelon.	Total in each Division
18-pounder rounds per gun	172	73	27	13,392.
4.5-inch rounds per gun.	108	48	66	2,664. for 12 Hows.
				3,552. for 16 Hows.
S.A.A.		1,008,000	832,000	1,840,000.
Grenades.		4,140	1,380	5,520.

(c)

Under the present system, the following personnel and vehicles are employed in a Division for Ammunition Supply. Figures approximate only.

Detail.	Personnel.							Horses.						
	Officers.	Warrant Officers.	Clerks.	Staff Serjts. & Serjeants	Artificers.	Trumpeters.	Rank & File.	Total.	Riding	Draught.	Heavy draught	Pack.	Total.	Bicycles	Motor Cycles
Old System.															
3 F.A.Bde.Ammn.Columns.	12	3		15	24		402	456	60	516			576		
How.Bde.Ammn.Col.															
(3 batteries).	2	1		3	7		77	90	15	88			103		
Divnl. Ammn. Column.	11	4		8	30		468	521	46	590			636		
Attached.	1			3			4	8	5				5		
	26	8		29	61		951	1075	126	1194			1320		
New System.	16	5		28	39		722	810	90	920			1010		
Nett Saving	10	3		1	22		229	265	36	274			310		

VEHICLES.

	Ammn. Wagons.	L.G.S.	G.S.	Maltese.	Water.	Bicycles.
Old System.	60	15	131	1	6	9
New System.	60	15	87	2	3	14
Nett reduction.			44		3	
Increase.				1		5

Appendix 2.

O.C.

    D.A.C.

With reference to the scheme for the reorganization of the Ammunition Columns, please carry on out the formation of No.4 Section ("B" Echelon) forthwith. (This should be done by transferring 256 other ranks and 334 mules from the present 3 Sections of the Column.)

The movement should be completed by 5 p.m. Wednesday 17th. May 1916.

Captain F. PAVEY will take command of No.4 Section.

                                                        Captain, R.A.

15 5.1916.   Staff Captain, 38th. Divisional Artillery.

Appendix 3.

O.C.

Re... the reorganisation of the D.A.C., please arrange for the transfer of the undermentioned details from your Brigade Ammunition Column.

The Officer in charge should report to the O.C. D.A.C. at point L.25.b.8.10. at 8.30 am on 18th May 1916.

The move must be completed by 5 pm. 18th May 1916.

As these details are likely to remain in this Divisional Artillery they should be specially selected.

119th)
120th) B.A.C's will hand over to O.C. D.A.C:-
121st)
122nd)

119th B.A.C.	120th B.A.C.	121st B.A.C.	122nd B.A.C.
1 G.S.Wagon & technical stores.	-do-	-do-	16-4.5"Q.F. AMN.WGNS
16-18 pdr.Q.F. Ammn. Wagons.	-do-	-do-	1 G.S.Wgn & tl.sts.
5 Wagons Limbered G.S.	-do-	-do-	1 Water Cart.
1 Officer.	-do-	-do-	1 Officer.
----------	1 B.S.M.	-----	-------
2 Sergeants.	-do-	-do-	1 Sergeants.
1 Farrier.	-do-	-do-	8 Gunners. ?
2 Shoeing Smiths.	-do-	-do-	52 Drivers.
1 Saddler.	-do-	-do-	104 L.D.Horses
1 Wheeler.	-do-	-do-	(complete in teams)
2 Corporals.	-do-	-do-	
2 Bombardiers.	-do-,	-do- ?	
20 Gunners.	-do-	-do-?	
56 Drivers.	-do-	-do-	
112 L.D.Horses (complete in teams).	-do-	-do-	

Captain R.A.

15.5.1916.   Stafff Captain, 38th.Divisional Artillery.

O.C.

D.A.C.

Forwarded for your information.

15.5.1916.   Stafff Captain, 38th.Divisional Artillery.

Captain R.A.

Appendix "4"

Orders by Lt. Col. G.W. Hayward R.H.
Comndg: 38th Div. Amm.n Column
Friday 26th May 1916

The surplus details of the 38th Divisional Artillery will move to CALAIS as detailed below:-

__Advance Party__ composed as under will parade at 1.30pm 27.5.16 and will proceed to WITTES, there to await the Main Body.

 2/Lieut C. Copp.
 Bdr. Pendleton & Hoyles.
 2 Drivers
 1 G.S. Wagon with four horses.

This party will carry rations & forage up to and for 28.5.16.

__Main Body__ under Command of Major B.P. Burroughs R.F.A will parade at 7am 28.5.16.

This party will move by march route to CALAIS, billetting at WITTES on night 28/29 May, and at RECQUES on 29/30 May

Three days rations & forage will be carried in addition to the unconsumed portion of the days rations & forage.

The following are the approximate details

Personnel

 3 Officers
 2 B.S.M.
 6 Sergeants (3 A.V.C)
 7 Corporals.
 4 Bombardiers.
 1 Farrier
 1 Shoeing Smith
 48 Other Ranks.

The O.C. should report on arrival at CALAIS to Commandant, Base Depot Camp.

All documents to be handed over to this officer.

1 Copy. R.A 38th Divn.
1 Copy. Major B.P. Burroughs R.F.A
1 Copy. War Diary
1 Copy. File.

    Capt R.H.A
    Adjutant 38 D.A.C.

WAR DIARY
of
INTELLIGENCE SUMMARY

(Erase heading not required.)

Army Form C. 2118

38th Div. Amm. Col. (W.A.C)

Place	Date	Hour	Summary of Events and Information	Remarks and references to Appendices
BOISBERGUES	28/6/16	10 pm	The Column moved from ST. MICHEL at 7 pm 27/6/16 and marched via RUELLECOURT – BUNEVILLE – SIBIVILLE – FRÉVENT – BOUQUEMAISON – HEM – OUTREBOIS to BOISBERGUES arriving at 4 am 28/6/16. The personnel of 38th Heavy Trench Mortar Battery are attached to the Column for the present. Major D.P. BURROUGHS left yesterday for new Ream Railhead at DOULLENS.	
MIRVAUX	1/4/16 1 pm		The Column moved from BOISBERGUES to MIRVAUX leaving the former place at 7 pm 30/6/16. The route was via MAITHEUX – MASFER – CANDAS – TALMAS – SEPTENVILLE – PIERREGOT. Arrived at MIRVAUX 6 am 1/7/16. The Division now forms part of the 2nd Corps, 4th Army.	Appx. II. Special Order of the Day by Div. Commr.

E.M. Stafford
Lt. Col. R.A.
Comdg. 38th D.A.C.

Army Form C. 2118

V of 7 June

WAR DIARY
or
INTELLIGENCE SUMMARY

(Erase heading not required.)

38th Div - Ammunl. Col. (W.A.)

Instructions regarding War Diaries and Intelligence Summaries are contained in F.S. Regs., Part II. and the Staff Manual respectively. Title Pages will be prepared in manuscript.

Place	Date	Hour	Summary of Events and Information	Remarks and references to Appendices
THIENNES	12/6/16	10 p.m.	We were relieved today by 61st D.A.C. and moved out from PONT RIQUEL at 6.30 a.m., the Column arrived at THIENNES at about 2 p.m. having marched via LESTREM – MERVILLE and LE SART. 'B' Echelon moved out from ROBERMETZ at 8 a.m. and joined the column at MERVILLE.	38 Ja. O.O. No. 16. Appendix 5 attached
	13/6/16	10 p.m.	No. 3 Section marched out this morning with the Ammunition Brigades under his Col. C.O. HEAD and H.G. PRINGLE to FLORINGHEM via LILLERS. This Section is to be detached until further orders.	Appendix 6 & 7 attached
AUCHEL	15/6/16	10 p.m.	The D.A.C. less No. 3 Section moved out from THIENNES at 8 a.m. this morning and marched to AUCHEL via LILLERS. 330 Company A.S.C. (less detachment) and 49th Mobile Veterinary Section have been attached for the march. The column arrived at AUCHEL at about 2 p.m.	Appendices 7 & 8 attached
ST. MICHEL	16/6/16	12 Mn.	The Column moved out of AUCHEL and marched to BERLES via OURTON – FRÉVILLERS – VILLERS BRULIN, arriving at 1 p.m. It was then discovered that we were intended to proceed to ST. MICHEL, the Column waited by R.A. Headquarters suffering from thirst, served by Divisional Head Quarter (see Appendices 9 & 9). The column halted in BERLES for one hour and then moved to ST. MICHEL via TINQUES, arriving at 4 p.m.	Appendices 7, 8, 9 & 10 attached
	17/6/16	10 p.m.	No. 3 Section rejoined the main party today from PENIN.	

Appendix 8. Copy No. 3

Operation Order No 1.

By Lt. Col. G. W. Hayward R.F.A.
Comdg. 38th. Div. Ammn. Column.

14th. June 1916.

38th. D.A.C. less one section.

330 Company A.S.C. less detachment.

Mobile Veterinary Section.

The Units named in the margin will march tomorrow 15th. June 1916 in the order shown.

Headquarters 38th. D.A.C. will march at 8 a.m. followed by Nos. 1. 2. and 4 Sections.

330th. Company A.S.C. will move from ST. FLORIS in time to join the Column at ST. VENANT at 9.40 a.m. They will march immediately in rear of No. 4 Section 38th. D.A.C.

Mobile Veterinary Section will join the Column at BUSNES at 10.40 a.m. and will march immediately in rear of 330 Company A.S.C.

The Column will halt at ten minutes to each clock hour commencing at 9.50 a.m. Officers Comdg. Units will see that their commands are well closed up and that March Discipline is preserved throughout the march.

A halt will be made for one hour at about 11.50 a.m. just N. of LILLERS.

Billeting parties of two mounted NCO's from each unit will report to Major B. P. BURROUGHS R.F.A. at the head of the Column at 12.30 pm.

38th. D.A.C. O.O. No 1 Continued.

Units will be met on arrival at AUCHEL by their Billeting Parties who will conduct Units to the Billets to be occupied by them. Units should occupy their Billets as expeditiously as possible in order to avoid blocking the rear of the column.

Map Sheet. No 5A Hazebrouck.

Each Unit will detail an orderly to report to D.A.C. Headquarters one hour after arrival at AUCHEL.

Units will forward by 6 p.m. a list of billets occupied by them, showing names of owners and numbers of Officers and men against owner's name.

Orders for drawing supplies will be issued on arrival.

ACKNOWLEDGE

[signature]
Capt. R.F.A.
Adjt. 38th D.A.C.

Issued at 12.10 pm.
Copies to:-
No 1 Sect. 38 DAC
No 2   "   "
No 4   "   "
330 Coy. A.S.C.
Mobile Vety. Section
File
War Diary
A.A. 38 Divn.

Secret.
M.67.

Map showing Distribution on Arrival.

L'ABBAYES DE NEUVILLE FM.
123 F. Co. R.E.

OSTREVILLE.
1 Bn. 113 Inf. Bde.

ORLENCOURT.
1 Bn. 113 Inf. Bde.

MONCHY - BRETON.
1 Bn. 115 Inf. Bde.
115 T.M. Batty.

BETHONSART.
1 Bn. 114 Inf. Bde.
114 M.G. Coy.

VILLERS CHATEL.
19th Welsh (Pioneers)
D.A.C.

MINGOVAL
1 Bn. 114 Inf. Bde.
1 Sec. 130 F. Amb.

113th INF. BDE. AREA.

ROCOURT ST LAURENT
330 Coy. A.S.C.
331 " "

MARQUAY.
1 Bn. 113 Inf. Bde.
113 T.M. Batty.

HERLIN - LE - VERT.
115 M.G. Coy.

CHELERS.
H.Q. 115 Inf. Bde.
1 Bn. " "
333 Coy. A.S.C.

GUESTREVILLE
151 F. Coy. R.E.

VILLERS BRULIN.
1 Bn. 115 Inf. Bde.
1 129 F. Coy. R.E.

115th INF. BDE. AREA.

114th INF. BDE. AREA.

ROELLECOURT.
○ D.H.Q.
○ D.A.D.O.S.

BAILLEUL - AUX - CORNAILLES
H.Q. 113 Inf. Bde.
1 Bn. " "
113 M.G. Coy.
129 F. Amb.

TINCQUETTE.
130 F. Amb.
2 Coys. Bn.-
115 Inf. Bde.

TINQUE.
1 Bn. 115 Inf. Bde.
(less 2 Coys.)
H.Q. Train.

BETHENCOURT.
1 Bn. 114 Inf. Bde.

SAVY.
H.Q. 114 Inf Bde.
1 Bn. " "
114 T.M. Batty.

GRAND CAMP.
H.Q. 119 Bde R.F.A.
120 " " less guns
121 " " in line.
122 " "
M. dium French Mortars.

○ ST. MICHEL
C.R.E.
A.P.M.
Sanity Sect.
A.D.M.S.
A.D.V.S.
Mob. Vet.

○ LABELLE ERINE
Salvage Coy.

N.
Not to Scale.

38th (Welsh) Division.
12.6.16

M A R C H   T A B L E (Contd)

Page 5.

DATE	UNIT	FROM	TO	VIA	REMARKS
15th June	DIVISIONAL HEADQUARTERS	ST VENANT	ROELLECOURT * ST MICHEL & LA BELLE EPINE	BRYAS	To arrive by 2 p.m.
	2nd Artillery Group				
	6 Batteries 18 prs. 2 Batteries 4.5" Hows. 330th Coy. A.S.C. less detachment Mobile Vety. Section. D.A.C. less 1 Section	ST VENANT	RAIMBERT AUCHEL CAUCHY	LILLERS	To arrive by 2 p.m.
16th June	2nd Artillery Group	RAIMBERT AUCHEL CAUCHY	GRAND CAMP Area except 330th Coy. A.S.C. to ROCOURT ST LAURENT MOBILE VETY. SEC. to ST MICHEL. D.A.C. to ~~GAMBINS~~ BERLES.	PERNES and BRYAS Via BRYAS BRYAS Via CURTON & FREVILLERS	To arrive by 12 noon.

* To ROELLECOURT :- D.H.Q. and D.A.D.O.S.
   To ST MICHEL :- C.R.E, A.P.M, A.D.M.S, A.D.V.S.
   To LA BELLE EPINE: Salvage Coy.

H.E. Pryce
Lieut. Colonel,
General Staff, 38th (Welsh) Division.

MARCH TABLE (Contd)

Page 2

DATE	UNIT	FROM	TO	VIA	REMARKS
14th June	115th Inf. Bde Group Under orders of G.O.C. 115th Inf. Bde.	POBECQ - CALONNE & ST VENANT Area	AUCHEL DIVION	LILLERS	Tail of Column to be at RAIMBERT by 2 p.m.
	115th Inf. Bde 151st Fd. Coy. R.E. 131st Fd. Ambnce. 333rd Coy. A.S.C. 19th (Pioneer) Bn. W.R. Sanitary Section Medium Trench Mortars		) RAIMBERT))))))	Units for MAREST and not to reach CAUCHY via ALLOUAGNE AUCHEL and AUCHEL. Units for MAREST via CHOCQUES - MARLES and CALONNE - RICOUART	MARLES before 2 p.m.
	113th Inf. Bde Group Under Orders of G.O.C. 113th Inf. Bde.	NONNEHEM Area	RAIMBERT MAREST FLORINGHEM CAUCHY		
15th June	115th Inf. Bde Group	RAIMBERT AUCHEL DIVION	Area round CHELERS, except 19th Pioneer Bn. W.R. to VILLERS CHATEL. Med. T.M's to GRAND CAMP & Santy. Sec. to ST. MICHEL	OURTON FREVILLERS } Via BRYAS	To arrive by 2 p.m.
	113th Inf. Bde Group	MAREST FLORINGHEM CAUCHY RAIMBERT	Area round BAILLEUL AUX CORN- AILLES	VALHUON & BRYAS and VALHUON and MONCHY - BRETON	To arrive by 2 p.m.

S E C R E T   MARCH TABLE (38th WELSH DIV. ORDER NO. 30)

DATE	UNIT	FROM	TO	VIA	REMARKS
12th June	38th Divn. Ammn. Sub-Park	St VENANT	ST MICHEL Sur TERNOISE	LILLERS - PERNES - ST POL	Will march full and report to XVIIth Corps Park
13th June	114th Inf. Bde Group Under orders of G.O.C. 114th Inf. Bde				
	114th Inf. Bde 130th Fd. Ambnce 124th Fd. Coy. R.E. 332nd Coy. A.S.C.	BUSNES Area	RAIMBERT AUCHEL CAUCHY	LILLERS	Tail of Group to reach RAIMBERT by 1 p.m.
	1st Artillery Group 6 Batteries 18 prs. 2 Batteries 4.5" Hows. Section D.A.C. Portion 330th Coy. A.S.C.	ST VENANT Area	DIVION MAREST FLORINGHEM	LILLERS	Head of Group not to reach RAIMBERT before 1 p.m.
14th June	1st Artillery Group	DIVION MAREST FLORINGHEM	~~BERLES CAMBLIGNEUL~~ except portion 330th Co.A.S.C. to HOCOURT ST. LAURENT	OURTON FREVILLERS ~~BERMONSANT~~ A.S.C. via BRYAS	To be clear of OURTON by 11 a.m. A.S.C. to arrive at 2 p.m. at destination
	114th Inf. Bde Group	RAIMBERT AUCHEL & CAUCHY	Area around SAVY, except 124th Fd.Coy to VILLERS BRULIN	OURTON and FREVILLERS	Not to arrive at OURTON before 11 a.m.

Appendix 9

SECRET   COPY NO. 17

38TH (WELSH) DIVISION ORDER NO. 30

Reference Maps :-   12/6/1916.
1/100,000, Sheets
5a, and 11.

1. The Division will march South to the Area between ST POL and SAVY between the 12th and 16th instant in accordance with the attached March Table.

2. Group Commanders will inform DIVISIONAL HEADQUARTERS when each day's move for their Group has been completed.

3. The 38th Divisional Supply Column will move in accordance with instructions to be received from the D.D. S. & T.

4. A map showing distribution of troops on arrival is attached.

5. Reports for DIVISIONAL HEADQUARTERS will be rendered to ST VENANT up to 9 a.m. on the 15th instant, and to ROELLECOURT after that hour.

   ACKNOWLEDGE

                                    H. E. Pryce
                                    Lieut. Colonel,
                    General Staff, 38th (Welsh) Division.

Issued at 6.30 a.m.

Copies to :-

G.O.C.	A.D.M.S.	38th Div. T.M.Offr.
G.S.	38th D.A.C.	XIth Corps
A.A. & Q.M.G.	38th Div. Train	Ist Corps
Signal Coy.	Camp Commandant	IVth Corps
C.R.E.	A.D.V.S.	XVIIth Corps
G.O.C., R.A.	D.A.D.O.S.	R.T.O. LA GORGUE
113th Brigade	A.P.M.	A.D.P.S. XIth Corps.
114th Brigade	S.S.O.	
115th Brigade	38th Div. Sub-Park	
19th Welsh Regt.	38th Div. Supply Col.	

Appendix 10 Copy no. 1.

Operation Order No. 2
By Lt. Col. G.W. Hayward R.H.A.
Comdg. 38th. Div. Ammn. Col.
15/6/16.

The 38th. D.A.C. less one Section will move in the undermentioned order via OURTON — TRÉVILLERS — VILLERS BRULIN to BERLES tomorrow 16th. June 1916.

    Head Quarters 38th. D.A.C
    No. 2 Section   — . —
    No. 1 Section   — . —
    No. 4 Section   — . —

The head of the column will move at 8 am.

Rations will be drawn tomorrow on the main cross roads RAIMBERT — FLORINGHEM and FERFAY — COUCHY A LA TOUR at 7.30 am. Bty. Q.M. Sergts. will meet N.C.O. i/c Supply Wagons at No 4 Section Horse lines at 6.30 am.

330th. Coy. A.S.C. will move to ROCOURT ST. LAURENT via BRYAS under the orders of O.C. Unit, but will not move till D.A.C. is clear of AUCHEL.

49th. Mobile Veterinary Section will move to ST. MICHEL via BRYAS but will not march off until 330th. Company A.S.C. is clear of AUCHEL.

ACKNOWLEDGE

Issued at 9.15 pm.

Copies to:- No 1 Sect. 38 D.A.C. / 49 M.V.S.
    No 2 —   — / File
    No 4 —   — / War Diary.
    330 Coy. A.S.C.

M. Mullen
Capt. R.H.A.
Adjt. 38th. D.A.C.

SPECIAL ORDER OF THE DAY.

BY

MAJOR-GENERAL IVOR PHILIPPS, D.S.O.,

COMMANDING 38TH (WELSH) DIVISION.

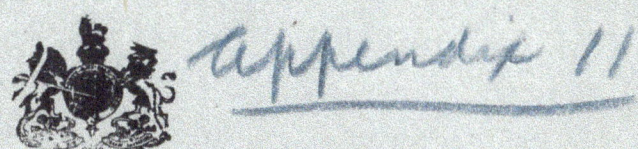

Wednesday, 14th June, 1916.

The Major General Commanding has much pleasure in publishing the following letter from the Corps Commander and his reply thereto:—

XITH CORPS.

The General Officer Commanding 38th Division:—

On the departure of the 38th Division from the XIth Corps, I should be glad if you will convey to all ranks my appreciation of their work since they have been in France.

From the time of its first arrival the Division has done well, both as regards fighting and administrative work. It has carried out five successful raids into the enemy's trenches, and has proved itself to possess a fine offensive spirit.

Great credit is due to you, your staff and commanders for producing this result. Colonel Pryce at the head of the General Staff, and Colonel Willes the chief of your Administrative Staff, with the Officers working under them, have shown exceptional knowledge and ability in the execution of their duties, and have made everything go smoothly and well for all with whom they have had to deal. I also appreciate the good work done by Colonel Morgan your A.D.M.S., and Major Hoare, A.S.C., your senior supply officer.

Brigadier-General Price-Davies, Commanding 113th Brigade; Brigadier-General Marden, Commanding 114th Brigade; Brigadier-General Evans, Commanding 115th Brigade, and Brigadier General Thompson, Commanding the Artillery of the Division, together with their staffs, have done everything in their power to create the fine fighting spirit which now exists in the Division, and have been loyally and willingly supported by commanding officers and all ranks of the units under their command.

The work of the Royal Engineers and Tunnellers, which has been of a most arduous nature, both in the front line and in the defences, communication trenches and drainage in rear, has been well carried out, and the exceptional ability and energy displayed by Colonel Atkinson, R.E., who has now left the Division on promotion, has materially advanced the efficiency of the Division in trench warfare.

I wish also to convey my thanks to your artillery group commanders, Colonels Paterson, Head, Pringle and Rudkin, each of whom has worked in the closest touch with the infantry commanders, and by their action, have been of the greatest assistance in securing the success of the various raids, and improving the moral of the Division.

My thanks are especially due to those gallant officers, non-commissioned officers and men of the following regiments who have successfully raided the German trenches, driven back the enemy in many hand to hand encounters, and proved themselves to be superior to the enemy in all respects:—

  15th R.W.F., under Col. Bell, raid on 7th May.
  10th Welsh Regt. under Col. Ricketts, who dug the Rhondda Sap on 27th May.
  16th R.W.F., under Col. Carden, raid on 31st May.
  14th R.W.F., under Col. Davies, raid on 4th June.
  10th Welsh Regt., under Col. Ricketts, who again distinguished themselves on
    the 4th June.
  14th Welsh Regt., under Col. Hayes, raid on 4th June.

Of the five raids no less than three were carried out by the 113th Brigade under the Command of Brigadier-General Price Davies.

Both I and my Staff regret that the Division is leaving the Corps, more especially considering the cordial relations and co-operation which have always existed between us. I am certain, however, that the Division will distinguish itself in its new surroundings, and will play a prominent part in defeating the enemy and winning the great victory which will bring the war to a successful conclusion.

(Signed) **R. HAKING**, LIEUT.-GENERAL,

12th June, 1916.   Commanding XIth Corps.

To Headquarters, XIth Corps:—

On behalf of every Officer, Non-commissioned Officer and man in the 38th (Welsh) Division, I desire to thank the Corps Commander most sincerely for his kind appreciation of our work. I can assure him that his remarks are most gratifying to us all.

We are proud to have received such praise and all ranks will accept it as a valueable proof that in their desire to make themselves efficient soldiers of the King they have not laboured in vain. It will also be a stimulus to all ranks to continue their efforts to qualify themselves to take their part in bringing the war to a victorius conclusion.

May I be allowed to add our appreciation of and thanks for the many kindnesses we have received from the Corps Commander and the Corps Staff. We have throughout our time in the Corps been helped to the utmost, and requests made by us for advice or assistance have always been met with a willingness and desire to help, which has lightened our task and added much to the pleasure of our work.

(Signed) **IVOR PHILIPPS**, MAJOR-GENERAL,

13/6/16.   Commanding 38th (Welsh) Division.

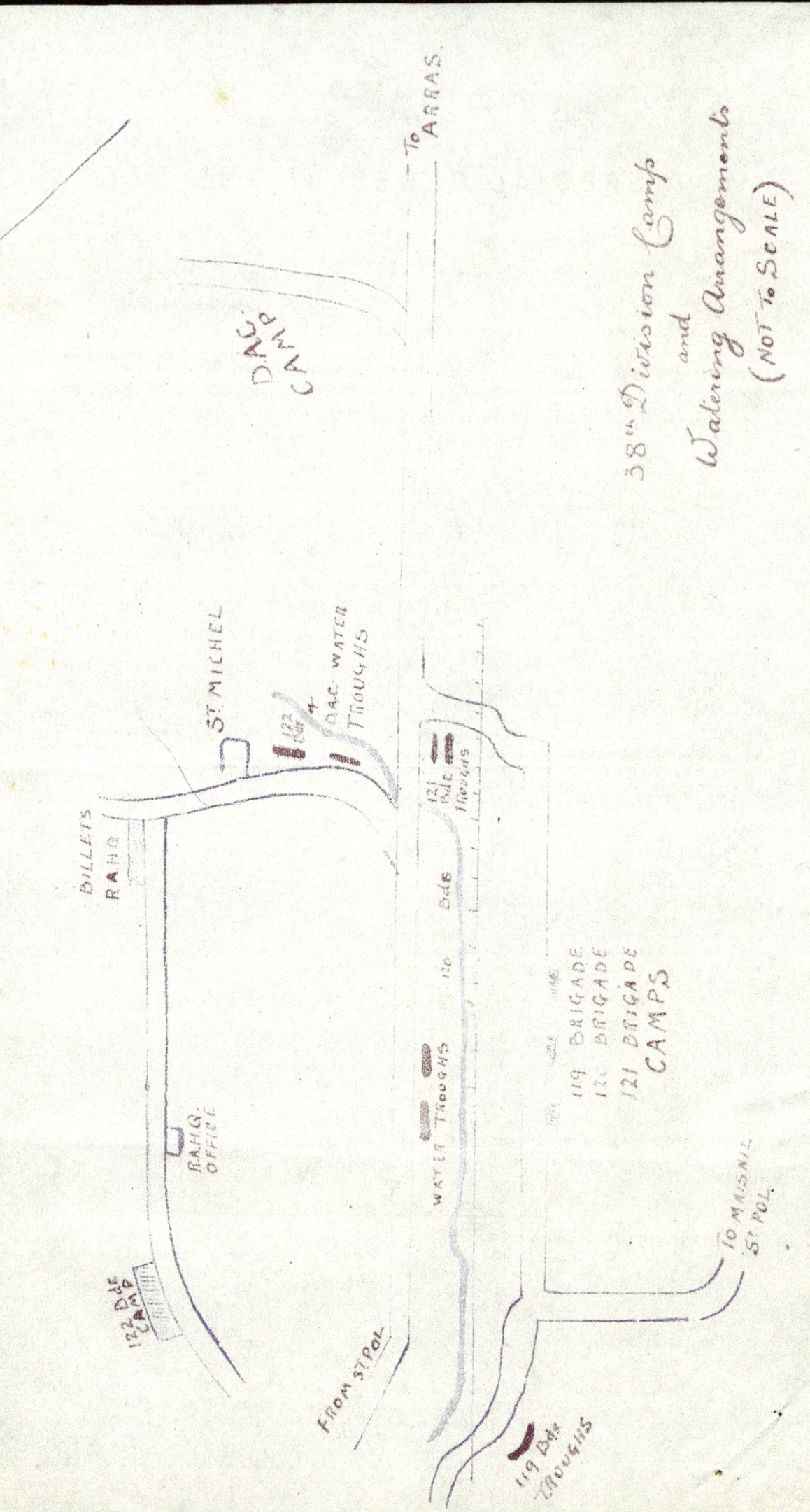

S E C R E T

MARCH TABLE (38th Divisional Artillery Order No. 17)

Date	Unit		From	To	Via.	Remarks
June 13th	120th Brigade H.Q.	)				The head not reach RAIMBERT before 1 p.m.
	"A"/119th	) Lt. Colonel				
	"B"/120th B/149	) C. O. HEAD				
	"C"/120th	) Commanding				
	"D"/120th	)	ST. VENANT	MAREST and NOYELLES FLORINGHEM	LILLERS	
	No. 3 Section "A" Echelon Divl. Ammn. Col. Detachmt 336 Coy A.S.C.					
	121st Brigade H.Q.	) Lt. Colonel				
	"A"/121st	) H.G.PRINGLE				
	"C"/121st	) Commanding				
	"A"/122nd	)				
	"D"/122nd	)	ST. VENANT	DIVION and FOSSE DE LA CLARENCE	LILLERS	
	(120th Brigade GROUP		MAREST	CAMBLIGNEUL billets East of road AUBIGNY - LES VENTS)))	OURTON - PREVILLERS and BETHONSART	To be clear of OURTON 120th by 10 am
June 14th.	121st Brigade GROUP		DIVION	CAMBLIGNEUL billet west of above road.))		121st by 9.30 a.m.

Sheet 2. Continued

Date	Unit	From	To	Via	Remarks
	H.Q. R.A. 38th Div.	ST. VENANT	FROLINGHEM	LILLERS	To be clear of RAIREST by
June 15th	H.Q. 119th Brigade "A"/120th Bde. B/120 "B"/119th Bde. } Lt. Colonel "C"/119th Bde. } PATERSON D.S.O. "D"/119th Bde. } Commanding	ST. VENANT	HAREST and NOYELLES	LILLERS	119th by 11.30 a.m.
	H.Q. 122nd Brigade } "B"/122nd Bde. } Lt. Colonel "C"/122nd Bde. } G.E.RUDKIN D.S.O. "B"/121st Bde. } Commanding "D"/121st Bde. }	ST. VENANT	DIVION and FOSSE DE LA CLARENCE	LILLERS	122nd by 12.15 p.m.
	Divisional Ammunition Column less one Section 330 Coy A.S.C. less detachment Mobil Veterinary Section	ST. VENANT ST. FLORIS BUSNES	AUCHEL	LILLERS	D.A.C. by 1 p.m.
	H.Q. 120th Brigade } } - H.Q. 121st Brigade }	CAMBLIGNEUL	(Divisional Area (in accordance (with attached Map.	AUBIGNY and SAVY	(Not to leave until (Btys. & section D.A.C. have been handed over to 51st Division
	H.Q. R.A. 8th Div.	FROLINGHEM	((Divisional Area (in accordance (with attached (Map	BRYAS, - OSTREVILLE and ST. MICHEL	To be clear of OSTREVILLE by
June 16th	119th Brigade Group	HAREST			119th by 10 a.m.
	122nd Brigade Group	DIVION			122nd by 10.30 a.m.
	Divisional Ammunition Column	AUCHEL			D.A.C. by 11 a.m.

SECRET   *Appendix 5.*   Copy No......8......

38th DIVISIONAL ARTILLERY.

OPERATION ORDER No. 16.

Reference Map Sheet 36 and 36 A. 1/40,000

1. The 38th Divisional Artillery will be relieved in the line by 61st Divisional Artillery and six reinforcing Batteries detailed by XIth Corps, between June 11th and 14th, and will move back into the ST. VENANT Area.
The relief will be carried out by sections.
The FAUQUISSART Group being relieved on the nights June 11th/12th and 12th/13th.
The MOATED GRANGE Group being relieved on the nights June 12th/13th and 13th/14th.
The details are shewn on table "A".

2. 38th Divisional Artillery will hand over guns complete to relieving Batteries under direct arrangements between Battery Commanders concerned with the following exception - In the case of 18 pdr., Batteries 38th Divisional Artillery Batteries will remove their No. 7 Dial Sights.

3. Relieving Batteries will hand over their guns complete with the above exception to 38th Division Batteries at the Wagon Lines.

4. All ammunition in the Dumps and gun pits at each gun position will be handed over to relieving Batteries.
This handing over will take place as under:-

       FAUQUISSART GROUP   at 12 noon, June 12th.
       MOATED GRANGE   "   at 12 noon, June 13th.

5. The 38th Divisional Artillery will move out of action with its ammunition complete to establishment.

6. The 38th Divisional Ammunition Column will be relieved by the 61st Divisional Ammunition Column on June 12th. The supply of ammunition for this Divisional area will be taken up by the 61st Divisional Ammunition Column at 6 a.m. on this date. The details of the relief will be arranged between the Officers Commanding, Divisional Ammunition Columns

7. Command of Groups will be handed over to the new Group Commanders on the completion of the Battery reliefs. Group Commanders will report to this Office by telephone that the relief is complete and that the Group has been handed over.

8. The G.O.C.R.A. 38th Division will hand over Command of the Artillery covering the MOATED GRANGE and FAUQUISSART Sections to the G.O.C.R.A. 61st Division on the night, June 13th/14th, on completion of relief

9. Headquarters R.A. 38th Division, will close at LA GORGUE at 10 a.m. June 14th and open at ST. VENANT, P.4.c.9.9. at the same time.
              A C K N O W L E D G E

June 10th 1916

Issued at 11 p.m.

                                     Captain R.A.
                      Brigade Major, 38th Divisional Artillery.

Copies to:-

38th Division "G"	121 Bde.R.F.A.	S.S.O.	R.A. 33rd Div.
-do- "Q"	122nd Bde.R.F.A.	A.D.M.S.	R.A. 35th Div.
R.A. XIth Corps	Divl.Amm.Col.	A.D.V.S.	R.A. 39th Div.
119th Bde.R.F.A.	38th Div.Signals	Staff Capt.	War Diary - 2
120th Bde.R.F.A.	38th Div.Train	R.A.61st Div.	File.

Appendix 6.

SECRET   R.A. 38th Div. No. G.S. 346.

O. C. ~~119th,~~
      ~~120th,~~
      ~~121st,~~ Brigade R.F.A.
      ~~122nd~~
      38th Divl. Amn. Column

1. Orders have been received that 6 - 18 pr., Batteries and 2 Howitzer Batteries will march down to the new area on the morning of June 13th.

   The eight Batteries who will be relieved by them will be formed into two composite Brigades as follows:-

   Lt. Colonel C.O. HEAD, 120th Bde. H.Q.   ("A"/119
                                                              ("B"/119
                                                              ("C"/120
                                                              ("D"/120

   Lt. Colonel H.G. PRINGLE,   ("A"/121
           121st Bde. H.Q.   ("C"/121
                                                              ("A"/122
                                                              ("D"/122

2. No. 3 Section, "A" Echelon, Divisional Ammunition Column, will be attached to these Brigades for ammunition supply and will march with them.

3. The march will take two days.

4. Further orders regarding this move will be issued later.

June 11th 1916
12.45 a.m.

                                                              Captain R.A.
                               Brigade Major, 38th Divisional Artillery.

Appendix 7.

SECRET   Copy No......8.

38th DIVISIONAL ARTILLERY

ORDER No. 17.

Reference Maps, Sheets 5 a., and 11   1/40,000
                  and Sheet 36 a.   1/40,000

1. The 38th Divisional Artillery will march South from the ST. VENANT Area in accordance with attached March Table.

2. The Batteries of the two composite Brigades and No. 3 Section, "A" Echelon, Divisional Ammunition Column, under Lieutenant Colonel C.O. HEAD and Lieutenant Colonel H.G. PRINGLE, will move into action on June 15th under orders of the 51st Divisional Artillery.

   The Battery Commanders of these Batteries will be sent forward on the morning of June 14th to report to Headquarters R.A., 51st Division for instructions.

   No. 3 Section "A" Echelon. Divisional Ammunition Column, will be attached for the march to Lieutenant-Colonel C.O. HEAD'S Brigade. Orders for its disposal will be issued by 51st Divisional Artillery.

3. The remainder of the Divisional Artillery will move into the Divisional Area North and West of ROELLE COURT.

4. Groups will march independently

5. The Medium Trench Mortars will march to GRAND CAMP in accordance with orders issued by G.O.C., 115th Brigade.

6. Reports for Headquarters R.A. will be rendered to P.5.b.2.9. (ST. VENANT) from 10 a.m. June 14th till 10 a.m. June 15th and to GRAND CAMP after this

                 A C K N O W L E D G E

June 12th 1916

Issued at

                                           Captain R.A.
                 Brigade Major, 38th Divisional Artillery

Copies to:-

38th Division "G"	38th Divisional Signals
-do- "Q"	38th Divisional Train
R.A. XIth Corps	S.S.O.
119th Bde. R.F.A.	A.D.M.S.
120th Bde. R.F.A.	A.D.V.S.
121st Bde. R.F.A.	R.A. XVIIth Corps
122nd Bde. R.F.A.	R.A. 51st Division
Divl. Ammn. Column	38th D.T.M.O.
115th Infy. Brigade	

SECRET

TABLE "A"

Date	Unit	Relieved by Unit	Div.	In action at	Wagon line at	Moves to	Remarks
Night June 11th/12th	One section "A"/122	One section "A"/308	61st	M.15.b.8.4.	R.10.c.4.8.	K.26.b.9.5.	
	-do- "B"/119	-do- "B"/308	61st	M.11.c.4.5.	R.4.d.2.2.	J.29.d.4.2.	
	-do- "A"/121	-do- "C"/158	35th	M.11.d.5.4.	G.33.d.2.5.	J.30.d.5.6.	
	-do- "A"/119	-do- "C"/174	39th	M.6.a.central	R.10.a.4.8.	J.29.c.8.3.	
	-do- "C"/121	-do- "B"/307	61st	H.34.a.9.5.	G.32.d.4.8.	K.26.a.5.8.	
	-do- "D"/120	-do- "D"/159	35th	H.6.a.5.10.	R.16.b.7.10.	J.36.c.8.1.	
	-do- "D"/122	-do- "D"/308	61st	I.10.c.5.8.	G.33.d.4.7.	K.26.c.3.2.	
Morning of June 12th.	H.Q. 120th Brigade	H.Q. 305th Bde.	61st	In rest at.	K.29.b.0.6.	J.27.d.7.6.	
	H.Q. 121st Brigade	H.Q. 307th Bde.	61st	In rest at	G.32.c.2.2.	LE SART	
	"C"/120 Brigade	"C"/307th Bde.	61st	In rest at	R.10.a.2.7.	J.28.a.6.5.	
	Divisional Amm.Column	Divisional Amm.Column	61st		R.3.b.8.6.	J.29.d.3.6.	
Night June 12th/13th	Remaining section "A"/122	Remaining section "A"/308	61st	As above	As above	As above	
	-do- "B"/119	-do- "B"/308	61st				
	-do- "A"/121	-do- "C"/158	35th				
	-do- "A"/119	-do- "C"/174	39th				
	-do- "C"/121	-do- "B"/307	61st				
	-do- "D"/120	-do- "D"/159	35th				
	-do- "D"/122	-do- "D"/308	61st				

SECRET

TABLE "A" Continued.

Date	Unit	Relieved by Unit	Div.	In action at.	Wagon line at	Moves to	Remarks
Night June 12th/13th	One section "A"/120	One section "B"/163	35th	M.16.d.5.8.	L.36.a.8.2.	P.1.c.8.2.	
	-do- "B"/122	-do- "C"/167	33rd	M.21.c.8.5.	R. 3.d.5.0.	J.21.d.9½.5.	
	-do- "B"/121	-do- "B"/306	61st	R.15.b.3.5.	R.5.c.2.6.	J.21.d.0.4.	
	-do- "C"/119	-do- "B"/305	61st	M.12.a.1.9.	R.16.a.8.9.	P.7.c.1.5.	
	-do- "B"/120	-do- "C"/306	61st	M.34.c.5.3.	R. 3.d.3.2.	P. 1.d.4.0.	
	-do- "C"/122	-do- "A"/306	61st	M.22.b.9.8.	G.31.b.5.1.	J.22.c.3.6.	
	-do- "D"/119	-do- "D"/306	61st	M.21.b.6.7.	M. 2.a.4.8.	M.21.d.9.2.	
	-do- "D"/121	-do- "D"/179	39th	M.10.d.5.5.	L.36.c.5.4.	J.21.c.3.5.	
Night June 13th/14th	Remaining section "A"/120	Remaining section "B"/163	35th	As above	As above	As above	
	-do- "B"/122	-do- "C"/167	33rd				
	-do- "B"/121	-do- "B"/306	61st				
	-do- "C"/119	-do- "B"/305	61st				
	-do- "B"/120	-do- "C"/306	61st	In rest at	R. 3.d.3.2.	As above	
	-do- "C"/122	-do- "A"/306	61st				
	-do- "D"/119	-do- "D"/306	61st	As above	As above		
	-do- "D"/121	-do- "D"/179	39th				
Morning of June 14th	H.Q. 122nd Brigade (Right Group)	H.Q. 306th Brigade	61st	M. 4.c.1.1.	---	J.21.d.2.4.	
	H.Q. 119th Brigade (Left Group)	H.Q. 308th Brigade	61st	M. 4.b.3.3.	---	P. 2.d.1.1.	

38th Div.
XV.Corps.

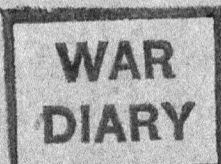

38th DIVISIONAL AMMUNITION COLUMN.

J U L Y

1 9 1 6

Attached:

Appendices 12 to
19 inc.

Army Form C. 2118

38 28th D.A.C. (not a,e) VOL 9

WAR DIARY
or
INTELLIGENCE SUMMARY
(Erase heading not required.)

Instructions regarding War Diaries and Intelligence Summaries are contained in F. S. Regs., Part II. and the Staff Manual respectively. Title Pages will be prepared in manuscript.

Place	Date	Hour	Summary of Events and Information	Remarks and references to Appendices
TOUTENCOURT	2/7/16		The Column left MIRVAUX at 12.30 a.m. today and marched to TOUTENCOURT via RUBEMPRÉ and HÉRISSART (map Sheet 11 Arras). We are in Bivouac in the woods above TOUTENCOURT. (See appr. 12)	appr. 12
TREUX	4/7/16		The Column left TOUTENCOURT at 10 p.m. 3/7/16 and marched to TREUX via CONTAY - FRANVILLERS - HEILLY - HALTE - MÉRICOURT (map sheet 11 Arras - 17 Amiens) the movement of together in the woods South of TREUX at 6 a.m. today. With orders of the Divisional Artillery are together in the woods. Ammunition supply for which is in TREUX. We now form part of the XIII Corps 4th Army. We provided a team today to view a captured German gun (77mm) which have been taken by the 7th Division.	appr. 13
---	5/7/16			
MÉAULTE	6/7/16		Today a spare section was formed from the existing sections of 'A' Echelon. This section is known as No. 6 Ord 'A' Echelon. It consists of 12 wagons Ammunition 18 pr. and four 4.5" How Bngrs. Two wagons G.S. per section has been handed over by No 4 Section to No. 1, 2, 3 & 5 Section. This wagons will contain 66 rounds of 4.5" Howitzer ammunition. Lieut. T. HAYES·SHEEN has been placed in command of No 6 Section with Lieut. P.R. DANGERFIELD to assist. This Section has been formed to supply the 119 H. Conigate. The Column left TREUX at 9 p.m. and marched to this place (E.21 d.) via VILLE-SUR-ANCRE (Sheet 62D) arriving at about 11 p.m. 3 wagons G.S. containing Mills Grenades and 16 wagons hundred G.S. containing S.A.A. marched	

1875 Wt. W593/826 1,000,000 4/15 J.B.C. & A. A.D.S.S./Forms/C. 2118.

WAR DIARY
INTELLIGENCE SUMMARY 38th D.A.C. (W.A.C)

Army Form C. 2118

Place	Date	Hour	Summary of Events and Information	Remarks and references to Appendices
MÉAULTE	9/7/16		...ed command of "Shiver". J.H. LLEWELLYN left TREUX at 8pm and proceeded to ORCHARD FARM CAMP at L.3 a 6.2 (Map Sheet 62 D). Shiver is taking charge of the Divisional Remt. Rtn. (See Appendix 14) The Column is now divided into two parts — No 1 & 2 Sections and half of "C" Echelon are attached to the 7th. D.A.C. and No. 3 & 5 Section with the other half of "C" Echelon are attached to the 21st. D.A.C. This has been rendered necessary as the 120th. and 121st. Brigades are attached to the 7th. Division in the case of the 119th. and 121st. Brigades are attached to the 21st. Division. In the case of the 120th. & 122nd. Brigades are now supplying direct to 50 gm. howrs if not over Brigades, obtaining ammunition through the 7th. D.A.C. — In the case of the 21st. Division, the Ammunition Wagons of 3 & 6" Sections are attached to the Brigades. They serve and are under their orders. The L.G.T. Wagons are employed in conveying ammunition from MÉAULTE Railway siding to a DUMP which has been established at LE CARCAILLOT FARM, the wagon lines of 119th. and 121st. Brigades drawing from thence.	Appx 14.
	12/7/16		Last night, Guns were sent to MAMETZ woods to remove four German Guns which had been captured by the 38th. Division. The woods were subjected to a very heavy shell fire which felled so many trees that it was impossible to get at the guns with the exception of one — a 77 m.m. Gun (Ansatz 1915 No 7374) (See Appx 15)	Appx 15.

Army Form C. 2118

WAR DIARY

INTELLIGENCE SUMMARY 38th D.A.C. (W.A.C.)

(Erase heading not required.)

Instructions regarding War Diaries and Intelligence Summaries are contained in F.S. Regs., Part II. and the Staff Manual respectively. Title Pages will be prepared in manuscript.

Place	Date	Hour	Summary of Events and Information	Remarks and references to Appendices
MÉAULTE	14/7/16		The party under Lieut. J.H. LLEWELLYN were withdrawn from ORCHARD FARM CAMP this afternoon.	
	15/7/16		2 S.A.A. Waggons under command of Lieut. J.H. LLEWELLYN assisted by Lieut. A.W. WILLIAMS proceeded to COIGNEUX via MÉAULTE - DERNANCOURT - MILLENCOURT - SÉNLIS - MEDANVILLE - FORCEVILLE - BERTRANCOURT. This party took with it 17 Waggons G.S. containing S.A.A. 3 Waggons G.S. containing Mills Grenades and 15 Waggons limbered G.S. containing S.A.A. Two Waggons containing "Pocha ett" belonging to Australian of the 115th Infantry Brigade accompanied the party. These "Pocha" were brought in tonight by two Waggons from F 17 b (Map Sheet 62 D) Lieut. T.J. JONES was sent to join the 12 2nd Brigade tonight.	Appx 16
	16/7/16		Twelve horses and three Drivers were sent tonight to B/122 Brigade to replace casualties. Four horses and seven Gunners sent to C/122 Bde. to replace casualties.	
ST. LEGER	18/7/16		The Column marched from MÉAULTE at 4 pm yesterday and marched to ST. LEGER via TREUX - MERICOURT - HEILLY - FRANVILLERS - CONTAY - HARPONVILLE - LEAVILLERS - LOUVENCOURT - BUS-LES-ARTOIS - COIGNEUX arriving at 5 am today.	Appx 17
	20/7/16		Headquarters D.A.C. moved today to COIGNEUX.	
COIGNEUX	21/7/16		An Ammunition Dump has been formed near COIGNEUX and all ammunition for the present will be supplied from there.	

Army Form C. 2118

WAR DIARY
INTELLIGENCE SUMMARY 38th. D.A.C. (W.A.C.)
(Erase heading not required.)

Place	Date	Hour	Summary of Events and Information	Remarks and references to Appendices
COIGNEUX	29/7/16		No. 3 Section, made up an S.A.A. Section today.	
	30/7/16		Two "Rides" of No. 3 Section (under 2nd Lt. J.S. ARNOLD and 2nd Lt. J.H. LLEWELLYN) moved to AUTHIELE. The other "Ride" under Capt. J. PLUMMER moved to BEAUVAL.	Appendix 18.
	31/7/16		Two "Rides" of No. 3 Section moved to DOULLENS and entrained for MOPOUTRE and ARQUES respectively, the remaining third moved to CANDAS and entrained for ST. OMER. No 5" Section has been broken up and the details have by-passes the Sections from which they were drawn. All ammunition has been supplies direct to the guns by the D.A.C. since arriving into this area. A congratulatory message has been received from the G.O.C, XV Corps Appendix 19. Corps on leaving the Corps. We are now doing to the VIII Corps, Reserve Army.	

E.M.Hayward
Lt.Col. R.A.
Comdg. 38th. D.A.C.

1875. Wt. W593/826 1,000,000 4/15 J.B.C. & A. A.D.S.S./Forms/C. 2118.

A P P E N D I C E S
12
13
14
15
16
17
18
19

"A" Form.
MESSAGES AND SIGNALS.
Army Form C. 2121.

TO { **Appendix 12**

38th Divisional Artillery Order No 1.

Reference LENS

1. Divisional Artillery will march to TOUTENCOURT and HARPONVILLE tonight according to attached March Table.

2. Locations Divisional Headquarters ACHEUX
   113th Brigade RAINCHEVAL and ARQUES
   114 " Brigade POUCHEVILLERS
   115 " LEALVILLERS

3. Reports of arrival and locations to R.A Headquarters on arrival of Units.

4. Billeting parties to meet Staff Captain at R.A. Headquarters at 9 pm.

5. R.A. Headquarters will close at PIERREGOT at 11 pm after this time reports to TOUTENCOURT.

Acknowledge.

From Issued at 9.0 pm July 1st 1916
Place
Time

Bn RA 38th Div

Unit	Starting point	Time of passing Starting point	Route
HQ RA	TOUTENCOURT	11.10 a.m.	RUBEMPRE
119 Bde	HAPONVILLE	11.30 a.m.	HERISSART
121 Bde	HAPONVILLE	12.0 midnight	TOUTENCOURT
122 Bde	TOUTENCOURT	12.30 A.M.	
120 Bde	TOUTENCOURT	1.0 A.M.	
DAC	TOUTENCOURT	1.30 A.M.	
33rd Div Coy ASC	TOUTENCOURT	2.30 A.M.	

Cross Roads just North of RUBEMPRE

"A" Form.   Army Form C. 2121.

MESSAGES AND SIGNALS.   No. of Message _____

Prefix	Code	m.	Words	Charge	This message is on a/c of:	Recd. at _____ m.
Office of Origin and Service Instructions.			Sent			Date
			At ___ m.		Service	From
			To ___			By
			By ___		(Signature of "Franking Officer.")	

Appendix 1 (written across)

TO   Secret

38th Divisional Artillery Order No 32.

AAA

Reference Sheets 11 LENS and 17 AMIENS 1/100,000

1. The Divisional Artillery will march South tonight to the woods South of TREUX according to march table.

2. Units are not to pass the line WARLOY-CONTAY-BEAUCOURT road until 9.30 pm and are to be clear of this line by 12.30 AM.

3. Field Companies R.E. and Pioneers will march in front of R.A. by the same route. This may affect hour of passing starting point.

4. Reports of arrival giving time and location of Units to R.A. Headquarters on arrival.

5. Reports to R.A. Headquarters line up till 9 pm after that to TREUX.

Issued at 6 pm July 3rd 1916.

Childerd

Capt.
B.M. R.A. 38 Div.

MARCH TABLE

Unit	To	Starting Point	Hour of passing starting point	Route	Remarks
H.Q.R.A	TREUX	Road junction 2 mile N.W. of VADENCOURT Church.	9.15 pm	CONTAY	Units marching from TOUTENCOURT must use the most easterly road from TOUTENCOURT to CONTAY.
120 Bde			9.30 pm	FRANVILLERS	
122 Bde	Wood South of TREUX		10. pm	HEILLY	
121st Bde			10.30 pm	HALTE	
119th Bde			11 pm	MERICOURT	
B.A.C.			11.30 pm		

"A" Form.
MESSAGES AND SIGNALS.
Army Form C. 2121.

Appendix 14

TO: O.C. Section
38th D.A.C. Order No 6.

Day of Month: 6/7/16

AAA

Reference Map Sheet 62D.

1. The 38th D.A.C. less 15 Wagons L.G.S. and 3 Grenade Wagons will be ready to move at 8.30 pm today. Head of Column will move at 9 pm.

2. Order of March – HQ 1. 2. 3. 5 & 4 Sections. Ten minutes intervals between Sections.

3. The route will be via TREUX – VILLE to a position S.W. of MEAULTE.

4. One Mounted N.C.O per Section to report to Adjutant at 8.30 pm.

5. 8 Wagons L.G.S & 1 Grenade Wagon each from Sections 1. 2 & 3 will move at 8 pm under Lieut A.A. MORRIS to ORCHARD FARM CAMP at point L 3 c 5.2 and report to 2Lt J.H. LLEWELLYN on arrival. This move will be completed by 4 am 7/7/16. Further instructions will be handed to 2Lt MORRIS before moving off. 1 NCO from Sections 1. 2 & 3 to accompany this party.

Time Issued at 5.45 pm

Adjt. 38 DAC

ALL SERVICES.

Requisition or Issue Voucher for Stores.

Received from }
Required " }
by } ———————— *Appendix 15* ———— the
for }
undermentioned Stores.

No.	Description.

Received from
38th Divisional Artillery
one captured German
Field gun (No 7374)

A.E.Brown
O.O. 4 Army Troops

12/7/16

Signature _____
Rank _____
Date _____

This portion of the Voucher to be retained by the Officer in charge of Stores.

N.B.—The necessary alteration should be made in the heading of this form according to the service for which it is required.

London: Printed for H.M. Stationery Office by Waterlow & Sons Limited.

Appendix 16

38th. D.A.C. Order No 7.

14/7/16

Reference Sheets 62ᴰ & 57ᴰ

1 A S.A.A. Section composed as under will move tomorrow at 7 am. under the command of Lieut. J.H. LLEWELLYN.

2 The Section will move to COIGNEUX via MÉAULTE – DERNANCOURT – MILLENCOURT – SENLIS – HEDAUVILLE – FORCEVILLE – BERTRANCOURT. It should arrive at COIGNEUX at 2 p.m.

3 Composition of Section.
    Lieut. J.H. LLEWELLYN (In command)
    Lieut. A.W. WILLIAMS
    B.S.M. LEWIS
    1 Corpl. each from 1. 2. & 3 Sections
    1 Bombr. — do —
    1 D. Smith — do —
    6 Gunrs. — do —
    6 S.A.A. Wagons from 2 & 3
    5 — do — 1
    1 Grenade Wagon from 1. 2 & 3
    5 Wagons L.G.S. 1. 2 & 3

4 5 Wagons containing kits to accompany the party. These will be horsed by No 4 Section and will be accompanied by an N.C.O. who will bring them back next day.

Issued at 9.30 p.m.

Capt. R.A.
Adjt. 38 D.A.C.

SECRET   Copy No...8......

38th DIVISIONAL ARTILLERY ORDER NO. 24

Reference:- Maps Sheet 11 LENS 1/100,000 and Sheet 17 AMIENS, 1/100000

1. The Divisional Artillery will march North today according to attached March Table.

2. All echelons will march full, any units deficient must take immediate steps to fill up from Divisional Ammunition Column and railhead.

3. A Representative from each Brigade, Divisional Ammunition Column and 330th Company, A.S.C., will meet the Staff Captain R.A. at ST. LEGER Church at 6 p.m. this evening.

4. Reports to R.A. Headquarters at TRENX up to 11.30 a.m. New location will be notified later.

ACKNOWLEDGE

                                                                          Captain R.A.

R.A., 38th Div.
Issued at   a.m. July 19th 1916. Brigade Major, 38th Divl. Artly.

Copies to:-
38th Division.	119th Brigade	122nd Brigade	
R.A. 48th Div.	120th -do-	Divl. Amm. Col.	
R.A. VIIIth Corps	121st -do-	38th Div. Train.	

S E C R E T

MARCH TABLE

Unit	To	Starting point	Time of passing starting point	Route	Remarks
120th Bde.	COUIN		4 p.m.	MERICOURT	From LOUVEN-COURT 120th, 119th and 122nd Bdes will march via AUTHIE; 121st Bde and Divl. Ammn. Column via BUS - LES ARTOIS.
119th Bde.	ST. LEGER	Road junction just West of in IVRUX	4.30 p.m.	HALES	
121st Bde.	COIGNEUX		5 p.m.	HEILLY FRANVILLERS	
122nd Bde.	ST. LEGER		5.30 p.m.	CONTAY HARPONVILLE	
D.A.C.	COIGNEUX		6 p.m.	LEALVILLERS	
350th Coy. A.S.C.	H.Q. Train		7 p.m.	LOUVENCOURT	

Appendix 18

38th D.A.C. Order No 10.

1. The S.A.A. Company as detailed will leave ST. LEGER at 10 a.m. 29/7/16 and march to BUS-LES-ARTOIS. A Billeting party of 1 Officer and 2 N.C.Os will report to the TOWN MAJOR at BUS by 9.30 a.m. and make arrangements for Billeting.

2. The Section will move on 30/7/16 as under:—

   1st Train. To AUTHIELE via THIÉVRES and must be clear of THIÉVRES by 11.15 a.m.

   2nd Train. As for 1st. TRAIN except that this party must be clear of THIÉVRES by 11.30 a.m.

   3rd. Train. To BEAUVAL via FRESCHEVILLERS and HULEUX.

   Billeting parties to be sent forward in each case.

3. The Section will move on 31/7/16 as under:—

	From	To	via	To arrive by	Train leaves at
1st Train	AUTHIELE	DOULLENS STATION	A 17 a 5.2 & A 16 b 3.8.	12.34 hours	15.34 hours.
2nd Train	AUTHIELE	DOULLENS STATION	A 17 a 4.6.	13.19 hours	16.19 hours.
3rd Train	BEAUVAL	CANDAS STATION	—	13.51 hours	16.51 hours.

The Railway journey will be about six hours. Rations must be distributed before leaving. There will be no halt to admit of this being done en route nor for watering Horses.

2 Canvas Buckets will be placed in each truck with the horses. Two or three men should ride in each Horse Truck.

Drag Ropes should be kept at hand for use as Breast lines in Horse Trucks.

4. Daily Casualty Returns will be rendered to this office by post. The O.C. No 4 Section will hand over his Censor Stamp until the section rejoins the Main Body.

Issued at 12.45 a.m.
29/7/16.

C.W.Mullin
Capt. R.F.A.
Adjutant 38 D.A.C.

Addenda to
38th. D.A.C. Order No 10

29/7/16.

1. A new copy of "Composition of Trains" is attached hereto and should be substituted for that already issued.

2. Portions of S.A.A. Section will entrain as under:-

   1st. Train at DOULLENS NORTH A10.d.8.2

   2nd. Train at DOULLENS SOUTH A16.b.8.8.

   3rd. Train at CANDAS.

   The Stations in each case must be reconnoitred beforehand.

3. Each portion of S.A.A. Section will travel with Brigade Groups as under and will detrain as shown:-

   1st. Train to 113 Infy. Bde. detrain at HOPOUTRE.

   2nd. Train to 114 Infy. Bde — ARQUES.

   3rd. Train to 115 Infy. Bde — ST. OMER.

4. Each portion will have a Wagon for Baggage and Supplies.

5. Units must be warned that the authority of the R.T.O. is paramount on all Railway property, also that, on detrainment, their Unit must be clear of the Station precincts before the next train comes in, irrespective of whether orders as to destination have been received or not.

6. One mounted N.C.O. will be detailed from each party as Billeting N.C.O. This N.C.O. should proceed with the first train party of the Infantry Brigade to which they are attached.

ACKNOWLEDGE.

Issued at 1 pm.

Adjt. 38 D.A.C.

S.A.A. Section 38 D.A.C.

Composition of Trains.

Details	1st Train	2nd Train	3rd Train	Total	Remarks
Officers	2	1	1	4	
W.O's	–	–	1	1	
Staff Sergts	1	–	–	1	
Sergts.	2	1	1	4	
Sergt. A.V.C.	1	–	–	1	
Corpls.	1	2	1	4	
Farrier	–	1	–	1	
S.S.	1	1	2	4	
Saddler	1	–	–	1	
Wheeler	–	–	1	1	
Gunners	13	13	14	40	
Drivers.	50	49	52	151	
Batmen	2	1	1	4	
Attached Drivers A.S.C.	1	1	1	3	
Rama	–	1	–	1	
Bomb Store Men	4	–	–	4	
Total all Ranks	79	71	75	225	
Horses:–					
Riding	6	5	5	16	
L.D.	98	96	100	294	
H.D.	2	2	2	6	
	106	103	107	316	
Vehicles–					
Wagons G.S. (S.A.A)	13	12	12	37	
— do — (Grenades)	1	1	2	4	
— do — (Baggage & Supplies)	1	1	1	3	
Wagons L.A.D.	5	5	5	15	Four Wheeled 59
Water Cart	–	1	–	1	Two Wheeled 1
	20	20	20	60	

Adjt. 38 D.A.C.

Appendix 19.

Fourth Army.

The C.R.A. and Divisional Artillery should know
of Corps Commander XV.C.C.'s letter for information of all
Canadian R.A.

              The 35th.Divisional Artillery leaves the XV.Corps
to-day. I am sorry to part with it. The Brigades have been
divided up under group commanders who were strangers to them,
but all arrangements have worked smoothly and the batteries
have answered to every call. They have occupied a forward
position in the recent operations under trying conditions and
have shot uniformly well. It is reported to me that all
ranks have displayed keenness, zeal and skill.

                                    sd. H.S.HORNE.
                                    Lieutenant General.,
                                    Commanding XV Corps.
H.Q. XV Corps.
18.7.1916.

O.C.
D.A.C.

The C.R.A. has much pleasure in forwarding above extract of a letter received from G.O.C. XV Corps for information of all concerned.

LRGaydn
Captain, R.A.
21.7.1916.   Staff Captain, 38th. Divisional Artillery.

WAR DIARY or **INTELLIGENCE SUMMARY** 36th D.A.C. (W.A.C.)

Army Form C. 2118

Place	Date	Hour	Summary of Events and Information	Remarks and references to Appendices
THIÉVRES	7/8/16		After handing over to GUARDS' D.A.C. the column moved to this place.	appx 20, 21 & 22
	8/8/16		X, Y & Z Medium & V/38 Heavy T.M. Batteries have joined for attachment during this move. (less 70 Rounds)	
BRÉTEL	10/8/16		The Column and Trench Mortar Batteries moved from THIÉVRES today and marched here via SARTON and DOULLENS. (less 103 Rounds)	appx 23 & 24
RUBROUCK	14/8/16		The D.A.C. and T.M. Batteries entrained at DOULLENS and CANDAS and detrained at ESQUELBECQ, CASSEL and ST OMER and marched to billets near RUBROUCK. No 3 Section is at VOLKERINGHOVE where they have been since coming into this area.	appx 25 & 26
	15/8/16		The S.A.A. Section has now ceased to exist as such and the Batteries have resumed their proper organisation. The T.M. Batteries have been detached and are now constituted under command of the D.T.M.O. In future all personnel of T.M. Batteries belong to D.A.C. and are detached for duty with T.M. Batteries. The establishment of D.A.C. has been increased by 15 Gunners so as to form a reserve for T.M. Batteries.	
Nr PESELHOEK A21 c 8.3 (sheet 28).	23/8/16		The column marched from RUBROUCK and VOLKERINGHOVE via WORMHOUDT, HERZEELE and POPERINGHE to this place in relief of 17th D.A.C. The position at Gun Positions. All ammunition drawn from a Corps Dump by D.A.C.	appx 27 28 & 29
	27/8/16		LIEUT. J.E. RANSLEY promoted CAPTAIN with effect from 27th January 1916. (London Gazette 25/8/16)	

Army Form C. 2118

WAR DIARY
or
INTELLIGENCE SUMMARY 38th. D.A.C (W.A.C)

(Erase heading not required.)

Place	Date	Hour	Summary of Events and Information	Remarks and references to Appendices
PESELHOEK	December 29/16		Lieut. K.K. HUGHES posted to Fourth Divisional Artillery.	
—	31/16		Lieut. S.H. HILDYARD posted to Fourth Divisional Artillery.	

E.G. Hayward
Comdg. 38th. D.A.C.

3/1/16

SECRET   Appy 20.   Copy No. 11

38th DIVISIONAL ARTILLERY ORDER NO. 28

1. The 38th Divisional Artillery will be relieved in the line after ~~daylight~~ dark on August 6th, 7th, and 8th. Our Right Group will be relieved by 6th Divisional Artillery on the nights 7th/8th and 8th/9th August. Our Centre and Left Groups will be relieved by Guards Divisional Artillery on the nights 6th/7th and 7th/8th August.

2. Batteries will be relieved by sections, one section relieving on each night.
Incoming Batteries will bring up their own guns complete.
38th Division Batteries will take their guns away complete.
The details of this relief are shewn on attached table.

3. Batteries of the Guards Division will take over all our wagon lines on the morning of the 8th.

4. Batteries and the Divisional Ammunition Column, 38th Divisional Artillery will move off from their present wagon lines with full echelons.

5. All maps 1/40,000 and 1/20,000 of the area, all ordinary and secret Trench Maps 1/10,000, defence scheme, aeroplane photographs and trench stores will be handed over to relieving batteries.

6. Guards Divisional Ammunition Column will relieve 38th Divisional Ammunition Column on the morning of August 7th This relief will be completed by 12 noon.

7. All ammunition in the gun positions will be handed over to relieving batteries and receipts taken.
Amounts handed over will be reported to this office as early as possible.
Batteries in Centre and Left Group will hand over their ammunition at 12 noon August 7th.
Batteries in the Right Group at 12 noon. August 8th.

8. Guards Divisional Artillery will be responsible for the supply and expenditure of ammunition in 38th Divisional Artillery Centre and Left Groups from 12 noon August 7th inclusive. 6th Divl. Artillery will be responsible for same in 38th Divl. Artillery Right Group from 12 noon August 8th inclusive

9. "Y"/38 and "X"/38 T.M. Batteries will be relieved by one section "Y" and "Z" Guards T.M. Batteries.
"Z"/38 will be relieved by a Medium T.M. Battery, 6th Division.
"V"/38 will hand over one gun to "Y"/Guards and one to "Z"/Guards.
Details of relief to be arranged between D.T.M.O's concerned.

10. Group Commanders will hand over command on completion of relief. This will be reported to this office and must be completed,

    Centre and Left Group by 12 midnight, August 7th.

    Right Group   -do-   August 8th.

11. G.O.C.R.A. Guards Division will take over command of Centre and Left Groups at 10 p.m. August 7th.

   G.O.C.R.A. 6th Division will take over command of Right Group at 10 a.m. August 8th.

   Reports to R.A. Headquarters, 38th Division at COUIN CHATEAU up to 10 a.m. August 8th.

12. Destination of 38th Divisional Artillery after relief will be notified as soon as possible.

13. A C K N O W L E D G E

Issued at 1 p.m. August 5th 1916

Geldard
Captain R.A.
Brigade Major, 38th Divisional Artillery

Copies to:-

R.A. XIVth Corps	119th Bde R.F.A.
20th Division	120 -do-
R.A. Guards Division	121st -do-
R.A. 6th Division	122nd -do-
R.A. 29th Division.	D.A.C.
38th Division	330th Coy. A.S.C.
38th Sub. Park.	

TABLE OF RELIEF

IN ACTION

58th Divl.Artly.	Relieved by	Remarks

RIGHT GROUP

Commander;- Lt.Col.
    P.J.PATERSON D.S.O.   6th Division

"B"/122nd
"C"/122nd
"B"/119th
"D"/119th

CENTRE GROUP
Commander;- Lt.Col.

C.O.HEAD	Lt.Col.F.C.BRYANT C.M.G.)	
	)	Guards
"A"/120th	"A"/76th)	
"B"/120th	"B"/76th)	Divisional
"C"/120th	"C"/76th)	
"D"/120th	"D"/76th)	Artillery
"A"/119th	"B"/61st)	
"C"/119th	"C"/61st)	

LEFT GROUP
Commander;- Lt.Col.

H.G.PRINGLE	Lt.Col.J.B.RIDDELL D.S.O.)	
	)	Guards
"A"/121st	"A"/75th)	
"B"/121st	"B"/74th)	Divisional
"C"/121st	"C"/74th)	
"D"/121st	"D"/75th)	Artillery
"A"/122nd	"A"/61st)	
"D"/122nd	"D"/74th)	

RELIEF OF WAGON LINES

120th Bde relieved by 76th Bde.
121st Bde   -do-   74th "
122nd Bde   -do-   75th "
119th Bde   -do-   61st "

"A" Battery being relieved by "A" etc., except in case of 119th Brigade which is relieved as follows;-

"A"/119 relieved by "B"/61
"B"/119   -do-   "A"/61
"C"/119   -do-   "C"/61

"D"/119 is not relieved.

Headquarters, 122nd Brigade relieved by Headquarters 61st Brigade on the morning of August 8th

----------o----------

Appx. 21.

O.C.
D.A.C.
———

With reference to 38th. Divisional Artillery No.28 dated 5.8.1916, Brigades and D.A.C. will take over Wagon Lines from the Guards Divisional Artillery according to attached list.

Arrangements should be made to send representatives to take over as early as possible.

All tents, shelters, bivouacs etc. taken over from 48th. Division must be handed over to incoming units and a list forwarded to this Office,

Chetwood
Captain, R.A.

5.8.1916.   Staff Captain, 38th. Divisional Artillery.

WAGON LINES.

R.A. Headquarters - BUS.

119th. Brigade R.F.A.

Brigade Headquarters located at THIEVRES.

"A"/119 take over "B"/61st. Brigade Wagon Lines.

"B"/119 "   " "A"/61st.   do   do

"C"/119 "   " "C"/61st.   do   do

"D"/119 Wagon Lines must be obtained. Guards D.A. have no "D" Battery.

120th. Brigade R.F.A. - AUTHIE.

Brigade Headquarters take over H.Q. 76th. Brigade.

"A"/120th. take over "A"/76 Brigade Wagon Lines.

"B"/120   "   " "B"/76   do   do

"C"/120   "   " "C"/76   do   do

"D"/120   "   " "D"/76   do   do

121st. Brigade R.F.A. - AUTHIE.

Brigade Headquarters take over H.Q. 74th. Brigade.

"A"/121 take over "A"/74 wagon lines.

"B"/121   "   " "B"/74   do   do

"C"/121   "   " "C"/74   do   do

"D"/121   "   " "D"/74   do   do

122nd. Brigade R.F.A. - ST LEGER.
Brigade Headquarters take over 75th. Brigade Headquarters.

"A"/122 take over "A"/75th. Bde. Wagon Lines.
"B"/122   "   " "B"/75th.   do   do
"C"/122   "   " "C"/75th.   do   do
"D"/122   "   " "D"/75th.   do   do

38th. Div. Ammn. Column. - THIEVRES.

Headquarters 38th.D.A.C. take over H.Q. Guards D.A.C.
No.1 Section take over No.1 Section Guards D.A.C.
No.2   "   "   "   No.2   "   "   "
No.3   "   "   "   No.3   "   "   "
No.4   "   "   "   No.4   "   "   "

Appx 22

38th D.A.C. Order No 11. d/6-8-16

1. The 38th D.A.C. will move to THIÈVRES tomorrow 7-8-16 as under:—

   No 1 Section at 8 a.m.
   " 2   "   " 9 a.m.
   " 4   "   " 9.30 a.m.
   Headquarters - 2 p.m.

   Sections will split up into small parties (no attempt must be made to march as a section) in order to avoid blocking the traffic.

2. N.C.Os & Men employed at the Dumps will rejoin their Sections in sufficient time to march with them, and work at the dump will be taken over by Headquarters detachment.

3. Units will hand over all billet stores in their possession to the incoming unit and take receipt for same. Such receipts to be forwarded to this office. A Representative with party will be left behind for cleaning up the Camp and handing over and will obtain Certificate as to cleanliness of billet, which will also be forwarded to this office.

4. No 4 Section will provide transport as usual for Trench Mortar Bty's rations. The N.C.O i/c will bring the transport to THIÈVRES as soon as he has delivered the rations. He will not collect any empty cartridge cases.

   Headquarter's rations will be retained by No 1 Section until arrival of H.Q. detachment.

5. All telephones will be handed into H.Q. Office at THIÈVRES tomorrow afternoon.

6. O/C No 2 Section will hand over to representative from Column H.Qrs three Units

Capt. R.H.A.
Adjt. 38 D.A.C.

appx 23

S E C R E T   Copy No. ....

38th DIVISIONAL ARTILLERY ORDER NO. 29

Reference Map 57 d. 1/40,000

1. 38th Divisional Artillery will march tomorrow to the HEM area according to attached march table.

2. Brigade billeting parties will meet a staff Officer R.A. at HEM Bridge A.7.d.7.8. at 7.30 a.m. tomorrow, August 10th.

3. Brigades and Divisional Ammunition Column will report their arrival and location of their Headquarters to R.A. Headquarters.

4. R.A. Headquarters will remain at DOULLENS. The location is A.17.c.1.5. and not A.17.a.1.0.

5. ACKNOWLEDGE

Issued at 5.45 p.m. August 9th 1916.   Captain R.A.
                                        Brigade Major, 38th Divisional Artillery

Copies to:-

R.A. XIVth Corps
XIVth Corps "G"
   -do-   "Q"
38th Division
119th Brigade - 5
120th   -do- - 5
121st   -do- - 5
122nd   -do- - 5
D.A.C.   - 4
330th Coy. A.S.C.
S.S.O. 20th Division.

MARCH TABLE

Unit	From	To	Route	Remarks
119th Bde.	THIEVRES		THIEVRES – ORVILLE – AMPLIER – AUTHIEULE – N.E. edge of DOULLENS – RISQUETOUT	Brigades will be clear of THIEVRES as follows:- 119th Bde by 7 a.m. 120th Bde by 7.30 a.m. 121st Bde by 8 a.m.
120th Bde.	AUTHIE			
121st Bde.	AUTHIE			
Divl. Ammn. Column	THIEVRES area	H.E.M Area	SARTON – thence by main road running nearly parallel to and South of river to DOULLENS Citadelle – BRETEL	Will be clear of SARTON by 8 a.m.
122nd Bde	ST. LEGER		AUTHIE – Road junction 300 yards South of THIEVRES Church – SARTON – thence by main road running nearly parallel to and South of river to DOULLENS Citadelle – BRETEL	Not to reach to AUTHIE until 7.30 a.m.

38th D.A.C. – Order No 12 d/9-8-16

Appy 24

1. The 38th D.A.C. will move to HEM tomorrow 10/8/16 as under:-
    - No 1 Section at 6 am
    - 2   "   "   6.15 am
    - 4   "   "   7 am
   followed by Headquarters.

2. No 1 Section will follow on behind No 2 Section on the THIEVRES – SARTON road and No 2 Sec. will lead the Column followed by Nos 1, 4 & H.Q.

3. The route to be followed is via SARTON, thence by Main road running nearly parallel to and south of River to DOULLENS Citadelle – BRETEL

4. The Column must be clear of SARTON by 8 am.

5. Billeting Parties consisting of 1 N.C.O and 2 Men from each Section will report to 2/Lt DANGERFIELD at No 2 Section at 5.30 am.

6. Camps will be left clean and ~~all Billet~~ the usual Certificate as to cleanliness obtained from the Town Major.
   Certificates will also be obtained from owners that they have no claims.

7. Representatives will attend at same time and place as usual for rations which will be brought on to new Billet.

C.W. Miller
Capt R.F.A
Adjt 38 D.A.C

R.A. 38th Div.No.G.S. 671

G.S.

D.A.C

Reference 38th Divisional Artillery Order No. 30 dated todays date.

In para 3, subpara commencing with Headquarters **Divisional Ammunition Column**, for "will entrain at **DOULLENS NORTH** and detrain at **ESQUELBECQ**" read "will entrain at **CANDAS** and detrain at **ST. OMER**"

Geddard

R.A. 38th Div   Captain R.A.
August 11th 1916.   Brigade Major, 38th Divisional Artillery

appy 25

SECRET   Copy No. XL

38th DIVISIONAL ARTILLERY ORDER NO. 30.

1. The 38th Divisional Artillery less one Section Divisional Ammunition Column and No. 330th Company, A.S.C. **will entrain at** DOULLENS NORTH A.10.d.8.2., DOULLENS SOUTH A.16.b.8.8. and CANDAS on 13th August 1916, in accordance with attached **time** table, marked "A"

   The stations must be reconnoitred before hand by representatives from each Brigade and Divisional Ammunition Column.

2. Troops must arrive at their entraining station **3 hours before** the time of departure of their train.

3. The 119th Brigade R.F.A. will entrain at DOULLENS NORTH and and detrain at ESQUELBECQ.

   The 120th Brigade R.F.A. will entrain at DOULLENS SOUTH and detrain at CASSEL

   The 121st Brigade R.F.A. will entrain at CANDAS and **detrain** at ST. OMER

   The 122nd Brigade R.F.A. less one Battery will entrain at DOULLENS NORTH and detrain at ESQUELBECQ
   One Battery 122nd Brigade R.F.A. will entrain at DOULLENS SOUTH and detrain at CASSEL

   Headquarters Divisional Ammunition Column, Trench Mortars and three quarters No. 1 Section Divisional Ammunition Column **will entrain at** DOULLENS NORTH and detrain at ESQUELBECQ

   One quarter No. 1 Section and No. 2 Section D.A.C. **will entrain** at DOULLENS SOUTH and detrain at CASSEL

   No. 4 Section will entrain at CANDAS and detrain at ST. OMER

4. Entraining Officers will be detailed to superintend the entraining as follows:-

   119th Brigade one Officer at DOULLENS NORTH
   120th   "   "   "   " DOULLENS SOUTH
   121st   "   "   "   " CANDAS

   They will report to the R.T.O. at their stations at least 3 hours before the hour of departure of the first train, and will join the last train of the 38th Divisional Artillery leaving their station and proceed to their destination.

5. Baggage, Supply and Hay Wagons will accompany Units full. Each Unit will entrain with current days rations in addition. Portion of Supply Column lorries will proceed loaded to new area.

6. The length of the railway journey will be about 6 hours. All food required during the journey by the men, or forage for the horses should be put in the railway trucks along with them. No halts, sufficiently long to distribute rations or water horses may be expected.

7. The following billeting parties:-

   5 Officers, 5 other ranks) Per R.F.A. Brigade
      10 horses   )

   1 Officer, 5 other ranks) Divisional Ammunition Column
      6 horses   )

   One representative   330th Company A.S.C.

   must be despatched by the first train from DOULLENS NORTH
   They will be met by the Staff Captain R.A. at detrainment
   station, who will hand to each unit a map showing billeting
   areas.

8. Units must be warned that the authority of the R.T.O. is
   paramount on all Railway property, also that, on detrainment
   their unit must be clear of the station precincts before the
   next train comes in, irrespective of whether orders as to
   destination have been received or not.

9. A C K N O W L E D G E.

Issued at 12 noon a.m. August 11th 1916

Captain R.A.

Brigade Major, 38th Divisional Artillery

Copies to:-
   R.A. XIVth Corps
   A.D.R.T. (III)
   119th Bde. R.F.A.   - 5
   120th Bde R.F.A.   - 5
   121st Bde R.F.A.   - 5
   122nd Bde R.F.A.   - 5
   D.A.C.   - 4
   330th Coy. A.S.C.   - 2
   38th Division
   R.A. VIIIth Corps

STRATEGICAL MOVE OF 38th (Welsh) DIVISIONAL ARTILLERY.

From. THIRD ARMY   via ST POL   To. SECOND ARMY

A. DOULLENS. N.   A. ESQUELBECQ

B. DOULLENS. S.   Hour H is at   B. CASSEL

C. CANDAS.   on   C. ST OMER

	Train No from Stations			SERIAL NUMBER	Date	Marche	Time of Dep:	Time due to arrive	Remarks.
	A	B	C						
1	2	3	4	5	6	7	8	9	10
				Billeting Parties (40 all ranks 40 Horses)					
	1	-	-	3802-3841- ~~xxxxxxxxxxxxxx~~	13/8	T.20	4.34		
	-	2	-	3850-3851-3880 One quarter	:	T.21	5.34		
	-	-	3	3860-3861-3862 One half.	:	T.22	5.51		
	4	-	-	3840-3842-3879 One quarter	:	T.23	7.34		
	-	5	-	3852-3880 One quarter	:	T.24	8.19		
	-	-	6	3862 Onehalf - 3863	:	T. 1	8.36		
	7	-	-	3843-3879 One quarter	:	T. 2	10.04		
	-	8	-	3853-3880 One quarter	:	T. 3	11.34		
	-	-	9	3864-3878-3896-3897-3898-3899	:	T. 4	11.51		
	10	-	-	3844-3879 One quarter	:	T. 5	13.19		
	-	11	-	3854-3880 One quarter	:	T. 6	14.19		
	-	-	12	3882 One third.	:	T. 7	15.06		
	13	-	-	3870-3871-3872 One half.	:	T. 8	16.19		
	-	14	-	3874.3879 One quarter.	:	T. 9	17.19		
	-	-	15	3882 One third.	:	T.10	17.51		
	16	-	-	3872 One half - 3873	:	T.11	19.34		
	-	17	-	~~xxxxxxxxxxxxxx~~ 3887	:	T.12	20.19		
	-	-	18	3882 One third	:	T.13	20.51		

SUMMARY.

    DOULLENS. N. (1)   6 T.Cs
    DOULLENS. S. (2)   6 T.Cs
    CANDAS   (3)   6 T.Cs

W. Gray

Lieut-Colonel

A.D.R.T. (III)

DOULLENS

August 7th 1916.

TABLE "D"

38th (WELSH) DIVISIONAL ARTILLERY.

UNIT.	SERIAL NUMBER	DESCRIPTION.
DIVISIONAL UNIT.	3802	H.Q. Divisional Artillery.
119th BRIGADE. R.F.A.	3840	Brigade H.Q.
	3841	"A" Battery.
	3842	"B" Battery.
	3843	"C" Battery.
	3844	"D" Battery. (How)
120th BRIGADE R.F.A.	3850	Brigade H.Q.
	3851	"A" Battery
	3852	"B" Battery
	3853	"C" Battery
	3854	"D" Battery (How)
121st BRIGADE R.F.A.	3860	Brigade H.Q.
	3861	"A" Battery
	3862	"B" Battery
	3863	"C" Battery
	3864	"D" Battery (How)
122nd BRIGADE R.F.A.	3870	Brigade H.Q.
	3871	"A" Battery
	3872	"B" Battery
	3873	"C" Battery
	3874	"D" Battery (How)
DIVISIONAL AMMUNITION COLUMN.	3878	H.Q. Divl Ammunition Column.
	3879	No. 1 Section Divl Ammn Col.) A.Echelon.
	3880	No. 2 Section Divl Ammn Col.)
	3881	
	3882	No. 4 Section Divl Ammn Col. B.Echelon.
	3896	Trench Mortar Battery (X. 38 R.A.)
	3897	Trench Mortar Battery (Y. 38 R.A.)
	3898	Trench Mortar Battery (Z. 38 R.A.)
	3899	Trench Mortar Battery (V. 38 R.A.)

3887 H.Q.&.H.Q.Coy Divisional Train

Order No 13. (continued)

One days rations and forage should be taken.

The N.C.O's should have full particulars of numbers of men and animals to be accommodated.

5. All Officers in charge of parties will make themselves thoroughly acquainted with 38th Dvn Order No 30, a copy of which has been issued to each Section.

6. A sufficient number of headropes should be provided with each party for use as breast lines in trucks. Four headropes per 8 horses should suffice.

7. ACKNOWLEDGE.

C.W.Mullen
Capt R.H.A
Adjt 38 D.A.C

Issued at 12.30pm
12/8/16
Copies to:-
2 X.38 T.M. Bty
3 Y 38   —.—
4 Z 38   —.—
5 V 38   —.—
1. War Diary
6 No 1 Section
7 2   —.—
8 4   —.—

Appy 26

38th D.A.C. Order No 13. Copy No 1
By Lt Col G.W Hayward R.F.A
Comm'dg 38 D.A.C.

1. The personnel of V/38 T.M. Battery will be attached for the move to Sections as under

Officers	Other Ranks	
2	20	to No 1 Section
-	20	to No 2 —"—
-	21	to No 4 —"—

   2/Lt HUGHES Y/38 T.M. Battery will be attached to No 2 Section.
   The whole of the above will report to Sections by 3 pm today. Any stores in possession should be distributed amongst the Sections for conveyance. Rations should also be handed over to Sections according to numbers attached.

2. A party comprised as under will parade at 10 pm tonight for loading duties at CANDAS station which should be reached by 12 midnight.
   Instructions have been issued to Lt HARRIS who will be in Command of the party:-

   Lieut HARRIS
   17 Other Ranks from X/38
   16   —"—   — Y/38
   17   —"—   — Z/38

   This party will take with them their rations for 13/8/16. Each Battery will supply one camp kettle.
   The party will leave by last train from CANDAS at 20.51 hours 13/8/16.

3. The remaining personnel of X, Y & Z T.M. Batteries with stores, will leave by Motor lorries at 6.30 am 13/8/16 for entrainment at CANDAS under Command of the Senior Officer with the party.

4. Billeting party as under will parade at H'dQrs wagon lines at 2.30 am tomorrow 13/8/16

   2/Lt P.R. DANGERFIELD
   1 Mounted Man from H'd Qrs.
   1   "   N.C.O   "   No 1
   1   "   N.C.O   "   No 2
   2   "   N.C.O's "   No 4

   over

SECRET   Copy No. 25

38th DIVISIONAL ARTILLERY ORDER NO. 31.

Reference Sheet 28 N.W. 1/20,000

1. 38th Division is relieving 4th Division on nights August 19th/20th and 20th/21st.

2. 38th Divisional Artillery will relieve 4th Divisional Artillery in the line during the nights August 21st/22nd and 22nd/23rd. The details of the relief are shewn on attached table.

3. Guns will be handed over complete in the pits. All sights, small stores, etc., belonging to the gun carriage being handed over.

    All secret and ordinary trench maps 1/10,000, air photographs, defence scheme and other papers and maps connected with the defence of the line will be handed over by outgoing units and receipts given for same.

4. Battery Wagon Lines will remain where they are until forward wagon lines are vacated by 4th Divisional Artillery. Orders for this relief will follow.

5. All ammunition in the gun positions will be taken over by Batteries of 38th Divisional Artillery at 12 noon, August 22nd. 38th Divisional Artillery will be responsible for ammunition expenditure after this hour.

6. All echelons 4th Divisional Artillery will move away full. To do this, they will take over ammunition from 38th Divisional Artillery as follows:-

    18 pdrs.   - 152 rounds per gun.
    4.5" Hows. - 96 rounds per gun.

    No. 4 Section, 38th Divisional Ammunition Column will hand over all 18 pdr., and 4.5" Howitzer ammunition to No. 4 Section 4th Divisional Ammunition Column.
    38th Divisional Ammunition Column will take over from 4th Divisional Ammunition Column two 15 pdr., guns and 200 rounds of ammunition.
    Receipts will be given and taken for all ammunition taken and handed over and the amounts reported to this office.

7. Orders for relief of Divisional Ammunition Column will be issued later.

8. The relief of the Medium Trench Mortar Batteries will take place on the night August 22nd/23rd, under arrangements to be made direct between D.T.M.O's. concerned.

9. Command of Groups will be taken over on completion of Battery reliefs.

10. G.O.C.R.A. 38th Division will take over Command from G.O.C.R.A. 4th Division at 9 a.m. August 23rd.

11. A C K N O W L E D G E.

[Signed]

R.A. 38th Division.
              Captain R.A.
          Brigade Major, 38th Divisional Artillery

Issued at 8 p.m. August 19th 1916.

Copies to:-

R.A. VIIIth Corps	122nd Bde. R.F.A. - 5
38th Division "G"	Divl. Ammn. Col. - 5
-do- "Q"	Signals
R.A. 4th Division	A.D.V.S.
119th Bde R.F.A. - 5	A.D.M.S.
120 " " - 5	Divl. Train
121st " " - 5	S.S.O.
330th Coy. A.S.C.	

TABLE OF RELIEFS

Date	Group	Unit 38th D.A.	Relieves		Position	Time	Remarks
21st.	Right	"B"/120th	88th Bty.	2 guns	B.29.a.0.0.		x "D"/32nd has 2 guns in each Group Each of these Sections is being relieved by a complete Battery. "D"/121st and "D"/122nd therefore will only hand over two guns each to the relieving Unit keeping two in their wagon lines until emplace- ments are ready for them.
"	"	"C"/120th	135th "	4 guns	B.29.c.4.5½.		
"	"	"C"/122nd	27th "	(3 guns	I.7.a.8.9. C.26.d.8.1.		
"	"	"A"/122nd	68th "	(1 gun (2 guns	I.2.c.7½.5½.	Relief not to take place before 9.30 p.m.	
"	"	"D"/120th	86th "	2 guns	B.29.c.7.9.		
"	"	x"D"/122nd	"D"/32nd	2 guns	H. 6.a.4.8.		
"	Left	"B"/121st	134th Bty.	(2 guns (2 guns (2 guns	B.14.b.9.2. B.15.b.7.7. B.16.c.7½.9.		
"	"	"C"/121st	127th "				
"	"	"A"/119th	125th "	(2 guns (2 guns (2 guns	B.22.d.1.8. B.22.a.9.2. B.28.b.7.6.		
"	"	"C"/119th	126th "				
"	"	"D"/119th	128th "	2 guns	B.22.d.2.5.		
"	"	x"D"/121st	"D"/32nd	2 guns	I.2.a.9½.5.		
22nd	Right	"B"/120th	88th Bty.	4 guns	B.29.a.0.0.		
"	"	"C"/120th	135th Bty.	2 guns	B.29.c.4.5½.		
"	"	"C"/122nd	27th "	2 guns	I.7.a.8.9.		
"	"	"A"/122nd	68th "	4 guns	I.2.c.7½.5½.		
"	"	"D"/120th	86th "	2 guns	B.29.c.7.9.		

Page -2-

Date	Group	Unit 38th D.A.	Relieves		Position	Time	Remarks
22nd	Left	"B"/121st	134th Bty.	2 guns	B.15.b.7.7.		
"	Left	"C"/121st	127th "	4 guns	B.21.b.3.5½.		
"	Left	"A"/119th	125th "	2 guns	B.22.d.1.8.	Relief not to take place before 8.30 p.m.	
"	"	"C"/119th	126th "	2 guns	B.28.b.7.6.		
"	"	"D"/119th	128th "	2 guns	B.23.c.0.5.		
"	Right	Lt.Col.RUDKIN D.S.O 122nd Brigade	Lt.Col.Lloyd D.S.O. 14th Brigade		H.6.b.4.6.		REIGERSBURG Chateau
"	Left	Lt.Col.PATERSON D.S.O. 119th Bde	Lt.Col.STIRLING 29th Brigade		B.28.a.6.1.		Chateau DE TROIS TOURS
?		121st Bde H.Q.	32nd Bde.H.Q.		PROVEN	Will be notified later.	
?		120th Bde H.Q.	---		Will be notified later	Will be notified later	
?		D.A.C. H.Q.	4th D.A.C.H.Q.		A.16.a.6.2.		
		No.1. Section	No.1 Section		A.21.b.4.7.	-do-	
		No.2 Section	No.2 Section		A.21.a.8.3.	-do-	
		No.3 Section	No.3 Section		A.21.a.9.8.	-do-	
		No.4 Section	No.4 Section		A.21.b.9½.5.	-do-	

R.A. 38th Div.No.B.M.25

In all orders and instructions regarding the forthcoming relief, while batteries are being used as 6 gun batteries,

"A"/119th and ½ "B"/119th will be called "A"/119th
"B"/121st and ½ "A"/121st will be called "B"/121st.

and so on.

(Sd) C. GELDARD.
Captain R.A.

R.A. 38th Division. Brigade Major, 38th Divisional Artillery.
19. 8. 16.

SECRET   R.A. 38th Div. No.G.S. 715

With reference to Order No. 31.

Para 6 (1st Part)

   152 rounds per gun 18 pdr.

   96   "   "   4.5" Howitzer.

These rounds, the contents of firing Battery and first line wagons, will be handed **over** by Batteries to Batteries relieved at the same time that 38th Divisional Artillery Batteries take over 4th Divisional Artillery Wagon Lines.

Para. 9

Group Commanders and Battery Commanders will take over Command of Groups and Batteries from 4th Divisional Artillery at **8 a.m. August 22nd**, instead of as therein stated.

                                                                                        Captain R.A.

R.A. 38th Div.

August 19th 1916   Brigade Major, 38th Divisional Artiller

Copies to:-

R.A. VIIIth Corps	D.A.C. - 5
38th Div. "G"	A.D.V.S.
-do- "Q"	A.D.M.S.
R.A. 4th Division.	Divl.Train
119th Bde - 5	S.S.O.
120th " - 5	330th Company A.S.C.
121st " - 5	Signals ½
122nd " - 5	

Appx 28

38th. DIVISIONAL ARTILLERY.
Relief of Wagon Lines and D.A.C.

1. The 38th.Divisional Artillery, less personnel now at Gun Positions, will relieve the 4th.Divisional Artillery between 2 p.m. and 4 p.m. on 23rd. August 1916, according to attached table.

2. Starting Point willbe Road Junction WORMHOUDT C.17.a.5.8. Units will march via HERZEELE - WATOU - POPERINGHE.

3. Ammunition will be handed over to the 4th.Divisional Artillery according to instructions contained in table.

4. All Units must arrive at their new Wagon Lines not later than 2 p.m. 23rd.August 1916.

5. Further instructions will be issued regarding the handing over of Guns and Howitzers.

ACKNOWLEDGE.

Issued at 2.15/pm

22nd.August 1916.

Captain, R.A.
for Brigade Major, 38th.Divisional Artillery

Copies to:-

R.A. Vlll Corps.
38th.Div. "G"
-do- "Q".
4th.Div.Arty.
119th.Bde.
120th.Bde.
121st.Bde.
122nd.Bge.
D.A.C.
etc.

Unit.	Relieves.	at	Time of Head of Column passing Starting Point.	Hand Ammunition to
120th.Brigade H.Q.	---	POPERINGHE.	6 a.m.	
"A"/120th.Brigade	38th.Battery	F.18.a.7.4.		68th.Battery.
"B"/120th.Brigade	38th.Battery	A.19.b.4.8.		38th.Battery.
"C"/120th.Brigade	127th.Battery	A.15.d.7.4.		127th.Battery.
"D"/120th.Brigade	36th.Battery	A.13.b.0.4.		36th.Battery.
119th.Brigade H.Q.	I.O. H.Q.	F.18.c.4.4.	4.30 a.m.	
"A"/119th.Brigade				125th.Battery.
"B"/119th.Brigade	128th.Battery	F.18.c.4.4.		68th.& 89th.Batteries.
"C"/119th.Brigade	126th.Battery	F.17.a.8.3.		126th.Battery.
"D"/119th.Brigade	128th.Battery	F.13.a.3.3.		128th.Battery.
122nd.Brigade H.Q.	R.G.H.Q.	A.19.b.1.9.	5.0. a.m.	27th.Battery.
"A"/122nd.Brigade				27th.Battery.
"B"/122nd.Brigade	27th.&	F.24.a.7.0.		127th.Battery.
"C"/122nd.Brigade	"D"/52nd.			"D"/52nd.Battery.
"D"/122nd.Brigade	Batteries.			
121st.Brigade H.Q.	32nd.Bde.H.Q.	F. 7.d.9.2.	5.30 a.m.	134th.Battery.
"A"/121st.Brigade				135th.Battery.
"B"/121st.Brigade	134th.and	F.24.a.5.6.		134th.& 135th.Batteries.
"C"/121st.Brigade	135th.			Keep.
"D"/121st.Brigade	Batteries.			
H.Q.36th.D.A.C.	H.Q.4th.D.A.C.	A.16.a.5.1.	6 a.m.	
No.1 Section	No.1 Section	A.21.b.6.2.		
No.2 Section	No.2 Section	A.21.a.8.3.		
No.3 Section	No.3 Section	A.16.a.7.6.		
No.4 Section	No.4 Section	A.21.b.9.5.		No.4 Section 4th.D.A.C.

Appx 29

38th D. A. C.   ORDER No: 12.

Reference Maps 27 and 28.

1. The 38th D.A.C. will move into Billets about A 27 (Sheet 28) tomorrow 23/8/16.

2. Route WORMHOUDT - HERZEELE - HOUTKERQUE - WATOU - POPERINGHE - PESELHOEK.

3. The Column will move in the order shewn below and will pass starting point at H.8 c 5-5. (Sheet 27) at the times shewn :-

   Headquarters D.A.C....... 4 a.m.
   No 4 Section............. 4-5 a.m.
   No 1 Section............. 4-25 a.m.
   No 2 Section............. 4-40 a.m.
   No 3 Section............. 4-55 a.m.

4. Head of Column will halt at D.18 a 10-5 at 6-50 a.m. for one hour for water and feed and breakfast.

5. Certificates to the effect that there are no claims against Sections, will be obtained from Billetees before leaving, and such Certificates forwarded to this Office in new area.

6. No 3 Section will send for ~~50,000~~ 60,000 rounds S.A.A. from No 4 Section this evening.

7. On arrival at new lines, No 4 Section will hand over to 4th D. A. C. all 18 pdr Ammunition and 12 Wagons of 4.5 Howitzer Ammunition.

Issued at 6.30 p.m.

[signature]
Capt R.F.A.
Adjutant 38th D. A. C.

WAR DIARY
or
INTELLIGENCE SUMMARY

38th D.A.C. (W.A.C)

(Erase heading not required.)

Army Form C. 2118

Vol. p. 8.

Place	Date	Hour	Summary of Events and Information	Remarks and references to Appendices
PESELHOEK	1/9/16		2Lieut. E.G. WELLS joined.	
"	6/9/16		2Lieut. R.K.T. GILES joined.	
"	15/9/16		2Lieut. A.M. WILLIAMS joined.	
"	22/9/16		2Lieut. A.M. WILLIAMS posted to 122nd Bde.	
"	26/9/16		Lieut. H.N. EPPENHEIM joined.	
"	27/9/16		2Lieut. F. WILLIAMS joined.	

Captain
2i/c for R.A.
Comdg. 38th D.A.C.

Army Form C. 2118

Vol 11

WAR DIARY
or
INTELLIGENCE SUMMARY

38th D.A.C. (W.A.C.)

(Erase heading not required.)

Instructions regarding War Diaries and Intelligence Summaries are contained in F.S. Regs., Part II. and the Staff Manual respectively. Title Pages will be prepared in manuscript.

Place	Date	Hour	Summary of Events and Information	Remarks and references to Appendices
PÉSELHERG	9/10/16		Lieut. H.N. EPPENHEIM and Lieut. F. WILLIAMS rejoined 24th Divisional Artillery	
---	17/10/16		Lieut. H.E. WELLS posted to Trench Mortars	
---	12/10/16		Lieut. R.W. DOBSON joined	
---	10/10/16		Lieut. W.L. BEHRENS joined.	

C.N. Heywood
Lieut. Colonel
Comdg. 38th D.A.C.

1/11/16

WAR DIARY

INTELLIGENCE SUMMARY 38th D.A.C. (W.A.C.)

Vol 12

Army Form C. 2118

Place	Date	Hour	Summary of Events and Information	Remarks and references to Appendices
PESELHOEK	9/16		Lieut. W. L. BEHRENS posted to 122 Bde. for attachment	Mdh
-do-	10/16		Lieut. R. G. HITCHINGS temporarily posted from 122 Bde.	Mdh
-do-	25/16		Lieut. W. T. GORNALL joined from T.M. Battery	Mdh
-do-	26/16		Lieut. P. K. T. GILES posted to T.M. Battery	Mdh

W. Maybury
Lieut. Colonel R.A.
Comdg. 38th D.A.C.

WAR DIARY
or
INTELLIGENCE SUMMARY 38th. D.A.C. (W.A.C.)

Army Form C. 2118

Place	Date	Hour	Summary of Events and Information	Remarks and references to Appendices
HERZEELE	15/12/16		The Column was relieved today by the 39th. D.A.C. at PESELHOEK. The distribution moved as shown in 38 DAC Order No 19 (appendix 31) attached. This place has been decided on as the "Rest Area" for the DAC and trick standings have been commenced by parties from 39th. Divisional Artillery.	Appx 30 & 31
HERZEELE	21/12/16		Capt. F. PAVEY struck off the strength on proceeding to England. Lieut. R.K. GREEN struck off the strength on being evacuated sick to England.	Nil
HERZEELE	31/12/16		A great deal of work has been done on the trick standings and much road improvement effected.	Nil

31/12/16

[signature]
Capt. R.E.
Comdg. 38th. D.A.C.

Appendix 31.

58th D.A.C. ORDER No: 19. dated 14/12/16.

Reference Map Sheets 27 & 28. 1/40,000.

1. The D.A.C. will move to Reserve Area at HERZEELE via PESELHOEK - SWITCHROAD - CROSS ROADS L.4.b.- WATOU - HOUTKERQUE on 15/12/16.

2. The following March Table will be rigidly adhered to. Parties will be clear of the Camp at the times shown against them.
   The first party must not cross the Starting Point, L.5.d.6.6. (Sheet 27), before 10 a.m.

    ½ No 1 Section under 2/LT: W.T.GORNALL............9-0 a.m.

1/3rd   4 Section under LIEUT: T.HAYES SHEEN........9-15 a.m.

    ½ No 3 Section under 2/LT: A.A. MORRIS...........9-30 a.m.

    Headquarters under OFFICER COMMANDING............9-45 a.m.

    ½ No 2 Section under 2/LT: A.W.WILLIAMS.........10-0 a.m.

    ½ No 1 Section under LIEUT: J.S.ARNOLD...........10-15 a.m.

1/3rd No 4 Section under CAPT: F. PAVEY..............10-30 a.m.

    ½ No 3 Section under CAPT: J.E.RANSLEY...........10-45 a.m.

    ½ No 2 Section under CAPT: J.PLUMMER.............11-0 a.m.

1/3rd No 4 Section under 2/LT: F.L. HYBART...........11-15 a.m.

3. REAR PARTY.
   Each Section will leave behind, a rear party consisting of B.Q.M.S. and 1 other mounted N.C.O. These will be brought on by the Adjutant.
   All Certificates etc. which are required for handing over will be left with B.Q.M.S.

4. COOKS.
   Cooks wagons and Cooks will proceed with the first party of each Section.

5. WAGON.
   O.C. No 4 Section will place One wagon and team at the disposal of H.Q., D.A.C. The wagon will be sent for today. The team will report at H.Q. by 9-30 a.m. 15/12/16.

6. CAMPS
   O.C. Sections will personally ascertain that their Camps are clean and tidy before leaving.

7. SICK.
   Any N.C.O. or man who is considered by the Medical Officer as unfit to proceed with his Section, will be sent to the Canteen by 11 a.m.

8. MARCH DISCIPLINE.
   An interval of 20 yards will be preserved after each six wagons.
   A N.C.O. will be posted in rear of each party and he will be instructed to ride back to the next party to give information in the case of a block. No party will on any account close up on the party in front of it.

(Continued)

38th D.A.C. ORDER NO: 19. d/14/12/16. (continued)

9. ORDERLIES.

   One Cyclist Orderly per Section will report to Column HdQrs: within One hour after arrival in new area.

10. BAGGAGE WAGONS.

    The Baggage wagons will arrive this evening. The will bring two days rations and forage. They will be rationed by Sections afterwards.

    The Baggage and extra Forage wagons which are joining this afternoon will parade on road near Column Headquarters at 7-30 a.m.
    They will proceed to new billets, unload, and then proceed to draw rations at HERZEELE by 10-30 a.m.
    The wagon for supplies for Trench Mortar Batteries should accompany this party.
    One man to act as Leader must accompany each wagon.

Issued at 11-45 a.m.

Capt R.F.A.
Adjutant 38th D. A. C.

AMENDMENT

to 38th D.A.C. ORDER NO: 19 dated 14th DECEMBER 1916.

1. **BAGGAGE WAGONS.**

   Reference Order No 10 of 38th D.A.C. Order No 19 d/14/12/16 paras 2, 3 and 4 are hereby cancelled and the following substituted:-

   Baggage wagons will march with the first portion of each Section.

   Rations will be drawn from the metre railway gauge station at HERZEELE at 3 p.m.

Issued at 12-45 p.m.

Capt R.F.A.
Adjt: 38th D. A. C.

Appendix 30

S E C R E T   Copy........24.....

38th DIVISIONAL ARTILLERY ORDER NO. 41

Ref:- Map Sheet 27 and 28 1/40,000

1. The 38th Divisional Artillery will be relieved in the line by the 39th Divisional Artillery during the nights December 14th/15th and 15th/16th.
   The present Left Group will remain in position.

2. The relief will take place by sections and guns will be handed and taken over complete with the Sights and stores laid down in the Handbook to be carried on the gun.
   Details are shown in the appendix.
   Completion of each Group relief to be reported by wire to this office.

3. The following advance parties will arrive on December 13th about midday and will be attached to the Units they relieve -

   Group Headquarters   -   1 Officer   6 men
   Batteries   -   1 Officer   6 men.

4. The following will be handed over to the incoming Units and receipts taken;-

   Trench and billet stores.
   All ordinary and secret maps of the forward area, scale 1/20,000, 1/10,000, and 1/5,000.
   Aeroplane photographs.

5. All ammunition at the gun positions at 12 noon, December 15th, will be taken over by 39th Divisional Artillery and receipts kept. The amounts handed over will be reported to this office by wire by 2 p.m. the same day. 39th Divisional Artillery will be responsible for ammunition supply after 12 noon, December 15th.

6. Ammunition expenditure up to 12 noon, December 15th will be reported by 38th Divisional Artillery, after this time by 39th Divisional Artillery.

7. 39th Divisional Ammunition Column will relieve the 38th Divisional Ammunition Column on December 15th. The 38th Divisional Ammunition Column will march to new area on the same day under separate orders from this office.

8. The relief of the Heavy and Medium Trench Mortars will take place on the 15th December under arrangements made direct between D.T.M.Os. concerned. The Heavy Trench Mortar and all stores connected with it will be handed over complete.

9. The 38th Divisional Artillery complete less Divisional Ammunition Column will proceed by march route to the Reserve Area on December 16th under separate orders   from this office.

-2-

10. The Command of the Divisional Artillery covering HILL TOP, LANCASHIRE FARM, and BOESINGHE Sectors will be handed over to The G.O.C.R.A. 39th Division at 8 a.m., December 16th.

11. Headquarters R.A., 38th Division will close at ST. SIXTE at 8 a.m. December 16th and open at ESQUELBECQ at 12 noon, the same day.

12 A C K N O W L E D G E

Sgd

Captain R.A.
Brigade Major, 38th Divisonal Artillery.

Issued at 11 a.m. December 12th 1916

Copies to:-

R.A. VIII Corps	119th Bde - 5	Signals
R.A. 39th Division	121st Bde - 5	A.D.M.S.
R.A. 55th Division	122nd Bde - 5	A.D.V.S.
5th Belgian Artillery.	Left Group	S.S.O.
38th Division "G"	D.T.M.O.	38th Div. Train.
38th Division "Q"	D.A.C.	

SECRET

APPENDIX

Unit	No. of Guns.	Position	Relieving Unit	Remarks
Right Group H.Q. 122nd Brigade.	-	H.6.b.2.4.	H.Q. 174th Brigade	"A"/121 and "A"/122 are not being relieved and will withdraw their guns to the Wagon Lines on the evening of December 15th. The ammunition in these pits will be taken over by "A"/186 in the case of "A"/121, and by "A"/174 in the case of "A"/122.
"C"/121.	6	I.7.c.8.9.	"A"/174	
"B"/122.	5	B.29.c.0.0.	"C"/174	
"C"/122.	4	B.30.d.2.5.	"B"/174	
x "C"/119. How.	4	B.29.c.7.9.	Section D/179.	x Relieved by 1 section only and will withdraw 2 guns to Wagon Lines on evening of December 15th.
"D"/122. How.	3	C.25.d.5.2.	"D"/174.	
Centre Group H.Q. 119th Brigade.	-	B.28.a.6.1.	H.Q. 186th Brigade	
∮ "B"/119.	(4 (2	B.28.b.8.6. C.26.c.30.15.	) "F"/186	∮ Enfilade section and one frontal section will be relieved on night 14th/15th.
"A"/119.	6	B.22.d.1.8.	"A"/186.	
"B"/121.	(3 (2	B.15.b.7.7. B.14.b.9.2.	) "C"/186.	
"D"/119. How.	(2 (1	B.22.d.7.1. B.23.c.0.5.	) "D"/186	
"D"/121. How.	4	I.2.c.8.2.	"C"/179.	

SECRET   Copy No. 21

38th DIVISIONAL ARTILLERY ORDER NO.42

Ref;- Maps Sheet 27 and 28, 1/40,000

1. 38th Divisional Artillery Wagon Lines will be relieved by the Batteries taking over the gun positions with the following additions;-

    "A"/121 will be relieved by "A"/179
    "A"/122 will be relieved by "B"/179.

    Brigade Headquarters Wagon lines as follows;-

    119th Brigade H.Q. will be relieved by 186th Brigade H.Q.
    121st Brigade H.Q.   "   "   "   "   179th Brigade H.Q.
    122nd Brigade H.Q.   "   "   "   "   174th Brigade H.Q.

2. The following arrangements are being made for taking over guns in exchange for those left in action.
    39th Divisional Artillery will leave the guns on their march through at HERZEELE, HOUTKERQUE and WATOU. They will be left under an escort at the side of the road, just East of these villages with trails pointing West, and should correspond in the case of each Battery with the number left in action.
    As the 39th Divisional Artillery have a great many guns at the I.O.M's Shop, they may not be able to carry this out completely. In these cases guns will be taken over by batteries from the I.O.M's Workshop as they become ready.

3. 38th Divisional Artillery will be located as follows in the Reserve Area -

    R.A.H.Q.   - ESQUELBECQ
    119th Brigade   - HOUTKERQUE
    121st Brigade   - WATOU   (Corps Reserve)
    122nd Brigade   - HERZEELE
    Trench Mortars   - HOUTKERQUE
    Divl.Amm.Column - HERZEELE

4. Units will move from the forward area with all echelons full.

5. Units will march as follows;-

    December 15th

    38th Divisional Ammunition Column.
        Route via PESELHOEK - SWITCH ROAD - Cross Roads L.4.b. - WATOU - HOUTKERQUE.
    The rear of the column must be clear of PESELHOEK before 12 noon.

    December 16th

    38th Divisional Artillery, less Divisional Ammunition Column.

    Route - HAMHOEK - SWITCH ROAD - thence same as Divisional Ammunition Column.

    Starting point L.5.d.6.6. where SWITCH ROAD joins POPERINGHE - PROVEN Road.

    Heads of Brigades will pass the starting point as follows;-

    122nd Brigade   -   9 a.m.
    119th Brigade   -   10 a.m.
    121st Brigade   -   11 a.m.

6. Seven lorries will be at STEENTJE FARM at 8 a.m. on December 16th to convey Trench Mortar Batteries to HOUTKERQUE.

7. Rear parties will be left behind and will rejoin their Units with clean billet certificate from incoming Units.

8. A C K N O W L E D G E

Gildard
Captain R.A.
Brigade Major, 38th Divisional Artillery

Issued at 3 p.m. December 12th.

Copies to:-

R.A. VIII Corps   Signals
R.A. 39th Division   A.P.M. 38th Division
R.A. 55th Division.   A.P.M. 55th Division.
38th Div. "G"   A.D.M.S.
38th Div. "Q"   A.D.V.S.
119th Brigade   - 5   S.S.O.
121st Brigade   - 5   38th Div. Train
122nd Brigade   5
D.A.C.
D.T.M.O.

SECRET G.S. No. 1241

CORRECTIONS TO
38th DIVISIONAL ARTILLERY ORDERS NOS. 41 and 42

1. Cancel para 9 of Order No.41 and substitute the following;-

    " The 38th Divisional Artillery complete less the Trench Mortars will proceed by march route to the Reserve Area on December 15th under separate orders from this office"

2. Cancel para 5 of Order No.42 and substitute the following;-

    5. 38th Divisional Artillery less the Trench Mortars will march to the Reserve Area on December 15th as follows -

    Route   SWITCH ROAD - Cross Roads L.4.b. - WATOU - HOUTKERQUE

    Starting point   L.5.d.6.6. where SWITCH ROAD joins POPERINGHE - PROVEN Road.

    Heads of Units will pass the starting point as follows;-

122nd Brigade	-	8 a.m.
119th Brigade	-	8.30 a.m.
121st Brigade	-	9 a.m.
Divl. Amm. Column	-	9.30 a.m.

3. Reference para 2 of Order No.42. "C"/119th Brigade will take over their two guns from "D"/179th Brigade at WATOU Church instead of outside HOUTKERQUE.

4. A C K N O W L E D G E

Childard

Captain R.A.

Brigade Major, 38th Divisional Artillery

Issued at 11.45 p.m. December 12th 1916

Copies to:-

R.A. VIII Corps	Signals
R.A. 39th Division	A.P.M. 38th Division
R.A. 55th Division	A.P.M. 55th Division
38th Div. "G"	A.D.M.S.
38th Div. "Q"	A.D.V.S.
119th Brigade - 5	S.S.O.
121st Brigade - 5	38th Div. Train.
122nd Brigade - 5	
D.A.C.	
D.T.M.C.	

WAR DIARY

INTELLIGENCE SUMMARY 38th D.A.C. (W.A.C.)

Army Form C. 2118

WM 14

(Erase heading not required.)

Instructions regarding War Diaries and Intelligence Summaries are contained in F.S. Regs., Part II. and the Staff Manual respectively. Title Pages will be prepared in manuscript.

Place	Date	Hour	Summary of Events and Information	Remarks and references to Appendices
HERZEELE	13/7/17		Instructions having been received to proceed with a reorganization of the D.A.C. the men personnel and horses, numbers 1 and 2 sections have been increased by about 50 horses each and about 20 more. They also have another Subsection each. No 4 Section has been reduced by 30 men and 12 horses and is numbered & will in future be known as No 3 Section. No 3 Section has become 119th (Army) Brigade Ammunition Column. It is officered by turning all S.A.A. away, and ammunition carrying held by No 1 & 2 Sections. This unit also has another Subsection. 915 strength in men and animals is slightly increased. For the present this unit remains attached to the D.A.C. for administration. Our 18th Ammunition Wagons and 3 GS Wagons arrived from 39th D.A.C. These vehicles have complete with teams and personnel being transferred from establishment to new establishment.	
[PESEL]HOEK	18/7/17		The D.A.C. and 119 B.A.C. returned today to their former location near PESELHOEK (Appendices 32 & 33 attached)	Appx 32, 33
---	23/7/17		Lieut. J.H. LLEWELLYN posted to 107 Battery [unclear] Aircraft	

Army Form C. 2118

WAR DIARY
INTELLIGENCE SUMMARY
(Erase heading not required.)

38th D.A.C. (W.A.C.)

Place	Date	Hour	Summary of Events and Information	Remarks and references to Appendices
PESELHOEK	25/7		2/Lieut. B.S. DORESA joined.	[appx]
–"–	25/7		2/Lieut. E.J. MILLER-WILLIAMS joined.	[appx]
–"–	25/7		2/Lieut. T.C.P. MULES joined.	[appx]
–"–	25/7		2/Lieut. H.C. ROWE joined.	[appx]
–"–	25/7		2/Lieut. R. RANK joined and posted to 38th T.M. Battery.	[appx]
–"–	27/7		No 1 Section 53rd D.A.C. attached for duty.	[appx]
–"–	27/7		Lieut. T.D. Williams appointed Divisional Bomb Store Officer (vice Llewellyn)	[appx]

10/7
Mr. Armytage Lt Col
Comdg 38th D.A.C.

Appendix 32

S E C R E T   Copy No. 16

38th DIVISIONAL ARTILLERY ORDER NO. 46

Reference Sheets 27 and 28 1/40,000

1. The 38th Divisional Artillery plus 119th Army Field Artillery Brigade will relieve the 39th Divisional Artillery in the Left Sector commencing January 17th. This relief will be completed by 8 a.m. January 19th.

2. Batteries will be relieved by sections, one section relieving on the night January 17th/18th and remainder of Battery on night January 18th/19th.
Guns in action will be taken over complete with all sights, and stores. Appendix "A" shows the details.

3. Headquarters, 119th Brigade and "A"/121 will each send an advance party of 2 Officers and 6 signallers to take over, these being the only two Units to take over new positions. They should arrive as early as possible on the morning of January 17th.

4. The following will be taken over by incoming Units and receipts given -

    Trench and billet stores.
    All ordinary and secret maps of forward area, scale 1/20,000, 1/10,000 and 1/5,000.
    Visibility Maps
    Panoramas
    Aeroplane photographs
    Defence and other Schemes, etc.

5. Ammunition at the gun positions will be taken over by 38th Divisional Artillery at 12 noon, January 18th. The amounts taken over will be wired to R.A.H.Q. by 2 p.m. on that day.

6. 38th Divisional Ammunition Column will take over ammunition supply from 39th Divisional Ammunition Column at 12 noon, January 18th.

7. The relief of the Heavy and Medium Trench Mortars in the line will be completed by 4 p.m. January 18th, the 38th Division Trench Mortar Batteries moving to the forward area on January 17th. The details will be arranged by D.T.M.O's concerned.

8. Relief of wagon lines will take place in accordance with Appendix "B".
All echelons will move full with the exception of "B" echelon, Divisional Ammunition Column, who will dump their ammunition at their present wagon lines.
This ammunition will be taken over by "B" Echelon, 55th Divisional Ammunition Column.
O.C. 38th Divisional Ammunition Column will arrange with O.C. 55th Divisional Ammunition Column to hand this over before leaving. The amounts handed over will be reported to this office.

/9.

9. The guns in our possession with the exception of "A"/122 will be handed over to 55th Divisional Artillery under orders which will be issued later.

10. G.O.C.R.A. will take over command of the Artillery in the Corps Left Sector at 10 a.m. January 19th.

11. Headquarters, R.A. 38th Division will close at ESQUELBECQ at 10 a.m. January 19th and open at ST. SIXTE at the same time.

12 A C K N O W L E D G E.

Issued at   5 p.m. 13.1.17.

Geldard
Captain R.A.
Brigade Major, 38th Divisional Artillery.

Copies to:-

119th Brigade   - 5
121st Brigade   - 5
122nd Brigade   - 5
D.A.C.   - 5
D.T.M.O.
R.A. VIII Corps
38th Div. "G"
38th Div. "Q"
R.A. 39th Division.
R.A. 55th Division.
5th Belgian D.A.
A.D.V.S.
A.D.M.S.
S.S.O.
D.A.D.O.S.
Divl. Train.
A.P.M. 38th Div.
A.P.M. 39th Div.
A.P.M. 55th Div.
Signals, 38th Divn.

SECRET

APPENDIX "A"

TO ACCOMPANY 38th DIVISIONAL ARTILLERY ORDER No.46

Unit	Relieves.	Position	No. of guns.	Remarks
Right Group Lt.Col. P.J.PATERSON D.S.O.				
122nd Bde. H.Q.	H.Q. 174th Bde.	H.6.b.2.4.		(1) "A"/122 will take their own guns into action on the evening of 17th January, the teams returning to present wagon lines.
(1) "A"/122.	---	I.2.c.7.6.	6	
"C"/121.	"A"/174	I.7.a.8.9.	6	(2) Will relieve on night January 17th/18th with section of old C/119
"B"/122.	"C"/174	B.29.a.0.0.	6	(3) D/122 will take up guns No.380 and 511 into action on night January 17th/18th. These to be manned by personnel of old C/119. This group of 4 guns will be commanded by Captain H.L.HYETT.
"C"/122.	"B"/174	B.30.d.2.5.	4	
(2) Section D/121 How.	Section D/174	B.29.c.7.9.	2	
(3) Section D/122 How.	Nil	B.29.c.7.9.	2	
2 sections D/122 How.	"D"/174	C.25.d.5.2.	3	Note:- At present there are three guns at B.29.c.7.9. Two will be taken over by section D/121. The other will be withdrawn by D/122 to its wagon lines by one of the teams bringing up guns No. 380 and 511.

Page 2.

Unit	Relieves	Position	No. of guns	Remarks
Centre Group. Lt.Col.H.G.PRINGLE D.S.O.				
H.Q. 121st Bde.	H.Q. 186th Bde.	B.28.a.6.1.	-	
(4) "B"/119	"B"/186	(B.28.b.8.6. (C.26.c.30.15.	4 2	(4) Will relieve a section in both positions on night January 17th/18th
"A"/119	"A"/186	E.22.d.1.8.	6	
"B"/121	"C"/186	(B.15.b.7.7. (B.14.b.9.2.	4 2	
2 section D/121 How.	"C"/179.	I.2.c.8.2.	4	
2 sections D/119 How.	"D"/186.	(B.22.d.7.1. (B.23.c.0.5.	2 2	
Left Group. Major J.E.MARSTON M.C. H.Q. 119th Bde.	H.Q. 179th Bde.	B.8.c.8.6.	-	
"A"/121	"A"/179	B.8.d.6.9.	6	(5) These two enfilade guns will be attached to A/121 and will relieve on night January 17th/18th.
(5) Section C/122.	Section B/174	T.21.a.85.25.	2	
"B"/179 becomes "C"/119 and remains at		B.8.b.90.25.	6	
Section D/179 Hows. becomes section D/119 and remains at		B.14.b.4.8.	2	

SECRET   APPENDIX "B"

         TO ACCOMPANY 38th DIVISIONAL ARTILLERY ORD.R.NO.46
         ----

1.   38th Divisional Ammunition Column will march to its old
     locations N.E. of PESELHOEK on January 18th.
     Route -
          WATOU. L.5.d.6.6. - SWITCH ROAD. A.26.a.5.2.

     The Head of the Divisional Ammunition Column to reach its
     destination by 12 noon.

2.   Owing to mange in our old wagon lines 38th Divisional
     Artillery will take over the wagon lines vacated by the
     55th Divisional Artillery.
     The Brigade Headquarters and Battery wagon lines will
     march on January 19th to their new wagon lines.
     Route -
          WATOU. L.5.d.6.6. - SWITCH ROAD.

     By 9 a.m. 122nd Brigade will be clear of WATOU
               121st Brigade will be clear of HOUTKERQUE
               119th Brigade will be clear of HERZEELE.

     Locations -

          122nd Brigade H.Q.   -   H.1.c.9.9.

                                         (A.26.a.8.3.
                 Batteries   (G.3.b.1.1.
                                         (A.28.c.4.5.
                                         (A.26.c.9.5.

          121st Brigade H.Q.   -   F.24.c.9.2.

                                         (F.24.c.9.2.
                 Batteries   (A.20.d.2.2.
                                         (A.20.c.6.3.
                                         (L.3.a.7.7.

          119th Brigade H.Q.   -   F.30.a.9.9.

                                         (F.27.d.8.0.
                 Batteries   (F.27.d.3.4.
                                         (E.21.a.5.9.

3.   All billet stores will be handed over here and taken over
     at the new locations and receipts given and taken.

O.C.

The following are the administrative arrangements in connection with the reliefs ordered in 38th.Divisional Artillery Order No.46 dated 13.1.1917.-

TRANSPORT. Motor Transport has been arranged for as under, for the purpose of conveying personnel from their present Wagon Lines to forward positions.

17th. January 1917.

  at 9 a.m.   7 Lorries at HOUTKERQUE for T.M. Batteries (one of these lorries must do a double journey) under order D.T.M.O.

  at 1 p.m.   4 Lorries at HERZEELE for 119th.Brigade ("A"/119th.Bde 2 lorries).

  at 1 p.m.   5 Lorries at HOUTKERQUE for 121st.Brigade ("D"/121st.Bde. 2 lorries).

  at 1 p.m.   5 Lorries at WATOU for 122nd.Brigade ("D"/122nd.Bde. 2 lorries).

18th. January 1917.

  at 1 p.m.   7 Lorries at HERZEELE for 119th.Brigade ("A"/119th.Bde. 1 Lorry).

  at 1 p.m.   9 Lorries at HOUTKERQUE for 121st.Brigade ("D"/121st.Bde. 1 lorry).

  at 1 p.m.   9 Lorries at WATOU for 122nd.Brigade ("D"/122nd.Bde. 1 lorry).

Lorries should be allotted to Batteries and move under Brigade arrangements.

Lorries should not be kept waiting longer than is absolutely necessary.

RAILHEAD etc.   Railhead for the Division on the 19th.inst. inclusive will be at PESELHOEK.

Refilling points will continue as at present until and including 18th.inst. and will be at PESELHOEK on 19th.

TRENCH and AREA STORES.   All Trench or Area Stores in present billets, in accordance with attached list, will be handed over to 55th.Divisional Artillery, and those of 55th.Division in forward area taken on charge.

            Lists/

-2-

Lists of all Stores handed over, or taken on charge, will be forwarded to R.A.H.Q. by 12 noon 21st. January 1917.

GUNS & STORES.

119th. Brigade will hand over guns to 277th. Brigade.
121st. Brigade   "   "   "   "   "   276th. Brigade.
122nd. Brigade   "   "   "   "   "   275th. Brigade.

Receipts for Guns and Stores handed or taken over must be obtained, and all deficiencies reported to this Office.

AMMUNITION.

Ammunition taken over at Gun Positions at 12 noon on 18th. inst. must be reported to R.A.H.Q. by wire by 2 p.m. and confirmed in writing by D.R.L.S.

Gun Positions will be supplied with Ammunition from their own Wagon Lines until all Wagons and Limbers have been emptied. Afterwards the supply will be from D.A.C. as was done formerly.

CAMPS & BILLETS.

In the event of no relieving unit arriving to take over present Camps and Billets, all area stores will be handed over to the permanent camp caretakers, and a report rendered to that effect.

An Officer must be left behind by each Brigade, D.A.C. and T.M. for 24 hours, for the purpose of enquiring into, and, if possible, settling all claims that may be preferred by the inhabitants.

Reports of vacation of land etc. must be forwarded to R.A.H.Q. by 12 noon 21st. January 1917.

J.R.Graystone.

Captain, R.A.
14.1.1917.   Staff Captain, 38th. Divisional Artillery.

Copies to:-
Staff Captain 38th. D.A.   A.P.M., 38th. Division.
      "   "   55th. D.A.   Control, POPERINGHE.
O.C. 38th. Divl. Train.   119th. Bde. R.F.A.
S.S.O., 38th. Division.   121st. Bde. R.F.A.
O.C. VIII Corps Ammn. Park.   122nd. Bde. R.F.A.
        38th. D.A.C. & D.T.M.O. 38th. Div.

LIST OF AREA STORES WHICH ARE TO BE HANDED OVER TO RELIEVING UNITS.

Camp Beds.
Chairs.
Forms.
Tables.
Benches.
Basins.
Buckets, fire.
    "   latrine.
Tanks water.
Pumps.
Lamps of all kinds.
Tarpaulins.
Bath tubs.
Wheelbarrows.
Handcarts.
Soyer Stoves.
Queen Stoves.
Primus Stoves.
Other Stoves.
Tents.
Tent Bottoms.
Canadian Tents.
Wringing Machines.
Washing Machines.
Gum Boots Thigh.
Fire extinguishers.
Miscellaneous.

LIST OF TRENCH STORES TO BE HANDED OVER ON RELIEF.

S.A.A.
Grenades.
Bombs.
Very Lights.
Rockets.
Food containers.
Gas Flapper Fans.
Horns Strombos.
Horns tenor.
Horns Claxon.
Horns Cylinders Compressed air.
Sniperscopes.
Vermorel Sprayers.
Rifle Grenade Stands.
Medicated blankets.
Bombers Shields.
Petrol Tins.
Trench Cookers.
Primus Stoves.
Gongs.
Trench Stretchers.
Washing Basins.

Snipers veils.
Snipers suits.
Gum Boots Thigh.
Trench Scoops.
Soyer Stoves.
Stoves, other patterns.
Braziers.
Bomb throwers.
Rifle Batteries.
Catapults.
Picks.
Shovels.
Sickles.
Mauls.
Saws.
Wheelbarrows.
Crowbars.
Scythes.
Pumps.
Axes.
Bill-hooks.
Wooden tubs.

S E C R E T Copy No......

AMENDMENT TO 38th DIVISIONAL ORDER NO. 46

1. Right Group will be commanded by Major D.C. STEPHENSON M.C. and not as therein stated.

2. Left Group will be commanded by Lieutenant Colonel P.J. PATERSON D.S.O. and not as therein stated.

3. ACKNOWLEDGE.

Major R.A.
Brigade Major, 38th Divisional Artillery.

Copies to:-

119th Brigade - 5
121st Brigade - 5
122nd Brigade - 5
D.A.C.   - 5
D.T.M.O.
R.A. VIII Corps
38th Div. "G"
  "   "   "Q"
R.A. 39th Div.
R.A. 55th Div.
5th Belgian Artillery.
A.D.V.S.
A.D.M.S.
S.S.O.
D.A.D.O.S.
Divl Train
A.P.M. 38th Div.
A.P.M. 39th Div.
A.P.M. 55th Div.
Signals, 38th Division.

appendix 33

38th D.A.C. ORDER NO: 20. dated 16th January 1917.

Map Reference. Sheets 27 & 28, 1/40,000.

1. MOVE.
   The 38th D.A.C. and 119 B.A.C. will move to their old locations N.E. of PESELHOEK on 17th and 18th January 1917, as under :-

2. ADVANCE PARTY.
   An advance party consisting of 2/Lt: A.W.WILLIAMS, 1 N.C.O from H.Q., 2 N.C.O's per section and 119 B.A.C., will parade with kits in the Square at 8-45 a.m. tomorrow 17th inst: to proceed to Forward area by motor lorry. The Senior N.C.O. of each section should be given a list of the stores which were handed over to the 39th D.A.C. Should there be any discrepancy between these lists and the stores handed over by the 39th D.A.C., N.C.O's concerned will immediately report the matter to 2/Lt A.W.Williams who will take steps to ascertain what has become of the missing stores
   2/Lt: A.W.Williams will report to the Adjutant for instructions before leaving HERZEELE.
   Rations, sufficient to last for breakfast on the 18th will be taken.

3. LOCATIONS.
   Sections and 119 B.A.C. will be located as under :-
   Headquarters & No 2 Section......A.21.a.8.3.
   No 1 Section....................A.21.c.7.7.
   No 3 Section....................A.21.b.6.4.
   119 B. A. C.....................A.21.a.8.7.

4. ORDER OF MARCH.
   The Column and 119 B.A.C. will move to PESELHOEK via HOUTKERQUE - WATOU - POPERINGHE on the 18th inst.
   Parties will pass the starting point at times stated as under :-
   Headquarters.........8 a.m.
   ½ 119 B.A.C.........8-15 a.m.
   ½ No 3 Section......8-30 a.m.
   ½ No 2 Section......8-45 a.m.
   ½ No 1 Section......9 a.m.
   ½ 119 B.A.C.........9-15 a.m.
   ½ No 3 Section......9-30 a.m.
   ½ No 2 Section......9-45 a.m.
   ½ No 1 Section......10 a.m.
   Starting point - Church corner, HERZEELE.

5. WAGONS.
   O.C. 3 Section will place wagons at the disposal of H.Q. & Section as under :-
   Headquarters......1 wagon.
   No 1 Section......2 wagons.
   No 2 Section......3 wagons.
   119 B.A.C.........2 wagons.
   These wagons should be sent for by O.C's to whom they are loaned, in the afternoon of the 17th inst: The teams will be sent up by O.C. 3 Section on the morning of the 18th inst:

6. REAR PARTIES.
   A Rear party consisting of the B.Q.M.S. and one other mounted N.C.O from each section and 119 B.A.C. will be left behind to hand over.
   The B.Q.M.S. should be furnished with all necessary papers. After handing over the B.Q.M.S. will report to 2/Lt: P.R.Dangerfield at Column Headquarters Officers Mess.

7. CERTIFICATES.
   The usual certificates as to cleanliness of billets, claims from Owners of billets, and receipts for billet stores will be handed to 2/Lt P.R.Dangerfield before the departure of the rear party.
   Certificates as to cleanliness of billets and receipts for billet stores should be in duplicate.

8. COOKS STORES.
   One wagon per section and 119 B.A.C. containing cooking utensils
   rations

38th D. A. C. ORDER No 20. continued.
----

rations etc: will parade on the Square in sufficient time to move off with Headquarters. The cooks should accompany these wagons.

O.C. Sections and 119 B.A.C. will report to the Adjutant when their Sections have arrived in the new area.

8. **TELEPHONES.**
One telephonist per Section and 119 B.A.C. will apply to Column Headquarters for a telephone on arrival in the new area.

Capt R.F.A.
Adjutant 38th D.A.C.

Issued at 8-30 p.m.
Copies to :-
　No 1 Section.
　No 2 Section.
　No 3 Section.
　119 B. A. C.

Army Form C. 2118

WAR DIARY
INTELLIGENCE SUMMARY 38th D.A.C. (W.A.C)

(Erase heading not required.)

Vol 15

Place	Date	Hour	Summary of Events and Information.	Remarks and references to Appendices
PESELHOEK	3/2/17		Lieut: H.C. ROWE posted to 119 (Army) B.A.C.	Nil
"	5/2/17		Capt. W.M. MATHESON joined and assumed command of "B" Echelon	Nil
			Lieut: F.L. HYBART posted at 121st Bde. R.F.A	
"	11/2/17		Lieut: T.F. BRIGGS joined from Base	Nil
"	18/2/17		Lieut: H. FOSTER (T.F.) joined from Base	Nil
"	25/2/17		The 119th (Army) B.A.C. ceases to be administered by 38 D.A.C. from this date.	Nil

1/3/17

Capt S Taylor RFA
45th Bde
Comdg 38th D.A.C.

Army Form C. 2118

WAR DIARY
or
INTELLIGENCE SUMMARY
(Erase heading not required.)

38th D.A.C. (W.A.C.)

Vol 6

Place	Date	Hour	Summary of Events and Information	Remarks and references to Appendices
PESELHOEK	1/2/17		Lt. Col. G.N. Hayward mentioned in despatches "London Gazette" 2nd January 1917.	
	14/3/17	9h.	2/B T. Clements joined from Base.	
	16/3/17	9h.	E.J. Miller-Williams posted to 38th Trench Mortar Battery.	
		9h.	H. Foster posted to 38th Trench Mortar Battery.	
	18/3/17	9h.	T.T. Briggs posted to 38th Trench Mortar Battery.	
	22/3/17	9h.	2/Lt. T. Liles joined from 38th Trench Mortar Battery.	
		9h.	to Leave joined from 55th Division.	
	28/3/17	9h.	2/Lt. Warren posted from 9/22 but not joined.	

1/4/17

[signature] Lt Col
Comdg 38th D.A.C.

Army Form C. 2118

WAR DIARY
or
INTELLIGENCE SUMMARY 38th D.A.C. (W.A.C.)
(Erase heading not required.)

Place	Date	Hour	Summary of Events and Information	Remarks and references to Appendices
PESELHOEK	23/4/17		2 Lieut. B.S. DORESA posted to 122 Bde. R.F.A.	With
			2 Lieut. C.N. FAIRBURN joined from 122 Bde R.F.A.	With
-do-	24/4/17		2 Lieut. P.K.T. GILES posted to 122 Bde. R.F.A.	With
			Divisional Brass Championship won by No 1 Section	
			No 1 Section placed first and No 3 Section placed fifth in Team Gun Competition.	

JK/17

E.M. Hayward Lt Col RFA
Comdg 38th D.A.C.

Army Form C. 2118

WAR DIARY
or
INTELLIGENCE SUMMARY
(Erase heading not required.)

38th D.A.C. (W.A.C.) Vol 18

Place	Date	Hour	Summary of Events and Information	Remarks and references to Appendices
PESELHOEK	6/5/17		Twenty-three 15 cm shells fell in and about the D.A.C. Lines during the hours 10.15 p.m. 5/5/17 and 4.20 a.m. 6/5/17. The objective was apparently the new railroad which has been laid near the camp. With the exception of one horse slightly wounded, there were no casualties. Horses were withdrawn to a flank and remained out of lines all night.	Apps 35
— do —	7/5/17		No. 2 Section moved out today to HERZEELE in order to make room for No. 1 Section 39th D.A.C.	
— do —	13/5/17		Temp. Lieut. P.R. DANGERFIELD promoted Temp. Lieut. Jany. 6th 1917 (London Gazette 11/59/17)	
— do —	17/5/17		Temp. Lieut. W. EVANS posted to Trench Mortar Battery X/38.	
— do —	18/5/17		Lieut. Col. G.W. HAYWARD and Lieut. (Temp. Capt) C.W.E. ALLEN mentioned in Despatches (London Gazette 9/4/17)	
— do —	21/5/17		No. 2 Section returned to PESELHOEK today and have been occupied in re-lines vacated by 19th (Army) F.A. Brigade.	Apps 36

Army Form C. 2118

WAR DIARY
or
INTELLIGENCE SUMMARY

38/h. Div. (W.A.E.)

(Erase heading not required.)

Instructions regarding War Diaries and Intelligence Summaries are contained in F. S. Regs., Part II. and the Staff Manual respectively. Title Pages will be prepared in manuscript.

Place	Date	Hour	Summary of Events and Information	Remarks and references to Appendices
PLOEGSTEERT	30/5/17		Lieut. W.A.F. GRAYSTONE posted to D/121 Bde. Lieut. J.D. ROBERTSON joined from D/121 Bde. Lieut. F. HORLINGTON joined from Base.	

1/6/17

M. Miller
Capt R.A.
Comdg. 38th. Div. Sac

1875 Wt. W593/826 1,000,000 4/15 J.B.C. & A. A.D.S.S./Forms/C. 2118.

SECRET. ~~*Appy 36*~~   Copy No. 19

38th. DIVISIONAL ARTILLERY OPERATION ORDER No.63.

1. On the nights 20/21st. and 21/22nd. May the 119th.(Army) F.A. Brigade will be withdrawn from the line and move to their present wagon lines. Reliefs as per table attached will take place.

2. On completion of relief Lieut.Colonel W.C.E.RUDKIN,D.S.O. will Command the Right Group consisting of :-

    122nd. Brigade.
    "C"/121.
    "D"/121. (less one section).

   Lieut.Colonel G.P.MacCLELLAN, D.S.O. will command the Left Group, consisting of :-

    "A"/121.
    "B"/121.
    1 Section "D"/121.

3. All Batteries will take their own guns into or out of action. Outgoing batteries will leave Aiming Posts to mark the Zero Line; incoming batteries will hand over a corresponding number.

4. Incoming Brigade Headquarters and batteries will send up parties of one Officer and three signallers per H.Q. and Battery to their new positions early on 20th.

5. All panoramas, visibility maps, papers connected with the defence of the line and area stores will be handed over by outgoing Headquarters and batteries, and copies of receipts forwarded to this Office.

6. Incoming batteries will account for Ammunition from 12 noon 21st. 119th. Brigade will move out and 122nd. Brigade and No.2 Section D.A.C. will move in with full echelons.

7. 122nd. Brigade will take over 119th. Brigade Wagon Lines on 22nd., "A"/122 from "A"/119 and so on. 119th. Brigade will then move back to the Camps now occupied by 122nd. Brigade North of WATOU. "A"/121 will take over the forward Wagon Line at STEENTJE from "A"/119 before noon on 21st.
   119th. B.A.C. and No.2 Section D.A.C. will exchange billets before noon on 21st.

8. Administrative Instructions with regard to the relief will be issued separately.

9. ACKNOWLEDGE.

   Issued at 4 p.m.
   16th. May 1917.

                                          J.E. Marston
                                          Major R.F.A.
                                 a/Brigade Major 38th. Divisional Artillery.

Copies to:-
R.A.,VIII Corps.	D.A.D.O.S.
38th.Div. "G".	A.P.M.
38th.Div. "Q".	A.D.V.S.
119th. Brigade - 5.	A.D.M.S.
121st. Brigade - 5.	S.S.O.
122nd. Brigade - 5.	38th.Div.Train.
D.A.C. - 1.	C.R.E.
D.T.M.O. - 1.	Signals.
R.A.4th.Belgian Div.	Officer i/c R.A.Signals.
R.A.39th.Div.	

TABLE OF RELIEFS.

Date.	Unit.	From.	To	Relieves.	Remarks.
Night 20/21.	1 Sect. "A"/122.	E.28.b.3.8.	Action at B.22.d.1.8.	1 Sect. "A"/121.	Teams and Limbers of 122nd.Brigade will return to Camps N.of TATOU after bringing guns up into action.
	2 Secs. "B"/122.	E.28.b.3.8.	" " B.28.b.8.6.) " " C.26.c.30.15.)	1 Sect. "B"/119. 1 Sect. "B"/119.	
	2 Secs. "C"/122.	E.16.d.8.3.	" " B.21.b.4.6.) " " B.14.b.9.2.)	1 Sect. "B"/121. 1 Sect. "B"/121.	
	2 Secs. "D"/122.	E.22.b.3.3.	" " B.22.d.20.45.) " " B.29.c.7.9.)	1 Sect. "D"/119 ~~121~~ 1 Sect. "D"/121 ~~119~~	
	1 Sect. "A"/121.	Action at B.22.d.1.8.	" " T.21.d.3.8.	1 Sect. "A"/119.	
	2 Secs. "B"/121.	" " B.21.b.4.6. " " B.14.b.9.2.	" " B.9.c.0.7.) " " B.15.c.2.9.)	1 Sect. "C"/119. 1 Sect. "C"/119.	
	1 Sect. "D"/121.	" " B.22.d.20.45	" " B.14.b.4.8.	1 Sect. "D"/119.	
	1 Sect. "A"/119.) 2 " "B"/119.) 2 " "C"/119.) 2 " "D"/119.)	Action.	Present Wagon Lines.		

TABLE OF RELIEFS Contd.

Date.	Unit.	From.	To	Relieves.	Remarks.
	122nd.Bde.H.Q.	E.28.b.3.8.	TROIS TOURS.	121st.Brigade H.Q.	Teams and Limbers of 122nd.Brigade will go to "B"/119.Wagon Lines F.18.c.4.7. and bivouac there for the night.
	121st.Bde.H.Q.	TROIS TOURS.	ELVERDINGHE CHATEAU.	119th.Brigade H.Q.	
	2 Secs. "A"/122.	E.28.b.3.8.	Action at B.22.d.1.8.	2 Secs. "A"/121.	
	1 Sect. "B"/122.	E.28.b.3.8.	" " B.28.b.8.6.	1 Sect. "B"/119.	
	1 Sect. "C"/122.	E.16.d.8.3.	" " B.21.b.4.6.	1 Sect. "B"/121.	
	1 Sect. "D"/122.	E.22.b.3.3.	" " B.22.d.20.45	1 Sect. "D"/119.	
	2 Secs. "A"/121.	Action at B.22.d.1.8.	" " T.21.b.2.4.	1 Sect. "A"/119.	
	1 Sect. "B"/121.	" " B.21.b.4.6.	" " T.21.a.9.2.	1 Sect. "A"/119.	
			" " B.8.b.8.2.	1 Sect. "C"/119.	
Night 21/22.	119th.Bde.H.Q. 2 Secs. "A"/119.	ELVERDINGHE CHATEAU (Action at T.21.b.2.4. (" " T.21.a.9.2.	Present Wagon Lines.		
	1 Sect. "B"/119.	" " B.28.b.8.6.			
	1 Sect. "C"/119.	" " B.8.b.8.2.			
	1 Sect. "D"/119.	" " B.29.c.7.9.			

ADMINISTRATIVE INSTRUCTIONS TO ACCOMPANY R.A. OPERATION ORDER NO.63.

dated 16-5-17.

1. On 21st May 1917 the 119th (Army) B.A.C. will move into Billets at present occupied by No.2. Section 38th D.A.C. at HERZEELE, (C12.b.9.4. Sheet 27), handing over their present Lines at A.21.a. 9.7. to No.2. Section 38th D.A.C.

   No. 2 Section D.A.C. will be clear of WATOU by 10.30 a.m. The 119th B.A.C. will be clear of present billets by 10 a.m.

2. ON 22nd Mayn 1917 the 119th Brigade (H.Qrs and Batteries) will exchange Wagon Lines and Billets with 122nd Brigade as follows :-

119th Bde. H.Qrs. relieve	122 Bde. H.Qrs.	at	E.28.b.3.8.	Sheet 27.
A/119	"	A/122	"	E.22.b.3.8.	" "
B/119	"	B/122	"	E.28.b.3.8.	" "
C/119	"	C/122	"	E.16.d.8.3.	" "
D/119	"	D/122	"	E.22.b.3.3.	" "
122nd Bde. H.Qrs.	"	119th Bde.H.Q.	"	F.18.c.4.4.	" "
A/122	"	A/119	"	F.18.c.4.6.	" "
B/122	"	B/119	"	F.13.c.4.7.	" "
C/122	"	C/119	"	A.13.b.1.5.	Sheet 28.
D/122	"	D/119	"	F.18.a.2.4.	Sheet 27.

   119th Brigade will be clear of point L.5.d.6.6. Sheet 27 by 10 a.m. and 122nd Brigade clear of WATOU by 10 a.m.

   A/121 relieves A/119 Forward Wagon Lines at A.17.d.9.3. before noon on 21st May and A/119 will move their Wagon Lines at F.18.c.4.6.

3. Lists of all Trench or Area stores handed and taken over in relief must be forwarded to this office by noon 23rd May 1917.

4. Ammunition at Gun positions will be handed over to incoming units at 12 noon 21st May.
   Amounts to be reported by Right and Left Group Headquarters to R.A.H.Qrs. by 2 p.m. 21st May.

5. Echelons will move with full establishments of ammunition and as far as possible with correct proportions, i.e. for 18-pr. ammunition 75% Shrapnel, 25% H.E.

6. The 38th D.A.C. will arrange to issue the necessary ammunition on 17th May 1917.

7. On 21st May No.2 Section D.A.C. will pick up supplies at HERZEELE and march to PESELHOEK
   119th B.A.C. will pick up supplies at PESELHOEK and march to HERZEELE.
   On 22nd May and subsequent dates No 2 Section D.A.C. will draw supplies at PESELHOEK and 119th B.A.C. at HERZEELE.
   All Wagons and horses of Divisional Train attached to No.2 Section D.A.C. will return to H.Q.Coy. Div. Train on 21st May 1917.

8. The 119th (Army) Brigade R.F.A. during their stay in Reserve Area will be rationed at HERZEELE by 39th Division by means of Light Railway in accordance with C.R.O. 1096 dated 25-4-17.

9. The Section of Headquarter Coy. 38th Divisional Train, at present attached to 122nd Brigade, will rejoin Divisional Train on 22nd May 1917.

10. Supplies on 22nd May for 119th Brigade Headquarters and Batteries will be picked up at PESELHOEK in the usual manner and delivered to CAMPS N. of WATOU, and on 23rd and subsequent dates from HERZEELE by 39th Division.

-2-

11. Horses for Baggage Wagons of 122nd Brigade will arrive at Battery Billets on the morning of the 22nd. The loaded wagons will march as a Train Column under R.A.S.C. arrangements, accompanied by a Baggage Guard in each case.
On arrival at the HAMHOEK LINES, the wagons will be kept in Wagon Lines for Battery use and horses will return to Divisional Train.

12. Advance parties should be sent by 119th B.A.C. and No.2 Section D.A.C. to take over Billets and Area stores on 20th May, and by the 119th Brigade Headquarters and Batteries and 122nd Brigade on 21st May.

13. A rear party will remain behind to hand over at each Wagon Line and Billet, and will not leave until a signed certificate is obtained from incoming unit that the billets and lines have been cleaned to their satisfaction. These certificates are to be forwarded to R.A.H.Q. as soon as reliefs are completed.

14. An officer from each Unit must remain behind in accordance with billeting rules to receive, and, if possible, settle all claims etc. before leaving.

15. Medical Arrangements.

A Medical Officer from 129th F.A. will look after 119th B.A.C. at HERZEELE.
A Medical Officer from 121st F.A. will look after Wagon Lines of 121st and 122nd Brigades.
Medical Officers of 119th, 121st and 122nd Brigades will remain attached to their own Brigade Headquarters.

JR Graystone

Captain R.A.
Staff Captain, 38th Divisional Artillery.

16-5-17.

38th Divisional Ammunition Column.   Order No 22.

1. On 21st May 1917, No 2 Section, 38th D.A.C. will move into Billets at present occupied by 119 (Army) B.A.C. at A.21.a.9.7. and will hand over their present billets at C.12.b.9.4. Sheet 27) to the last named unit.

2. No 2 Section will be clear of WATOU by 10.30 a.m.

3. List of all area stores handed and taken over in relief must be forwarded to this office by noon 22nd May 1917.

4. On 21st May, No 2 Section will pick up supplies at HERZEELE and march to PESELHOEK.

   On 22nd May and subsequently this Section will draw supplies at PESELHOEK.

   All wagons and lorries of Divisional Train will be returned to H.Q. Company, Divisional Train, on 21 : 5: 17.

5. Advance party should be sent to take over Area Stores from 119 (Army) B.A.C. on 20 : 5 : 17.

6. A rear party will remain behind to hand over billets and will obtain the usual certificates in duplicate from Incoming Unit and owner. These certificates will be forwarded to this Office by 6 p.m. 21 : 5: 17.

17th May 1917.

Capt R.F.A.
Adjutant 38th.D.A.C.

Copy No. 11

SECRET.

Appendix 35

38th. DIVISIONAL ARTILLERY OPERATION ORDER No.62.

1. On the nights May 4th./5th. and 5th./6th. 122nd. Brigade R.F.A. will be relieved in the line by the 174th. Brigade R.F.A. of 39th. Division and "C" Battery 121st. Brigade. Detail is shown in appendix "A".

2. Relief will take place by sections, one section being relieved on the first night and the remaining two on the second night, with the exception of "C" and "D" Batteries 122nd. Brigade. In these two cases the detached sections and one section in main position will be relieved on the first night, the remaining section on the second night.

3. 122nd. Brigade will take their own guns out of action and 174th. Brigade will bring their guns into action. Aiming posts will be left in the ground in all cases to mark the line of the guns.
The two O.P's at GOWTHORPE and the two at HILL TOP will be handed over to 39th. Divisional Artillery with all panoramas and visibility maps belonging to them.

4. On completion of Battery reliefs on the night May 5th/6th. O.C. 122nd. Brigade will hand over the present Right Group Hd.Qrs. with all papers and maps referring to 39th. Division Front to O.C. 174th. Brigade R.F.A.

5. The Ammunition in the pits at 12 noon May 5th. will be handed over to incoming Batteries. After this hour the 39th. Divisional Artillery will be responsible for the ammunition supply.
~~119th B.A.C. will hand over their lines at A.21.a.8.7. to a Section 39th.D.A.C. on May 5th. and will move back to HERZEELE.~~ No 2 Sect. 38 DAC will be relieved by No 1 Section 39th DAC on May 7th & move back to HERZEELE.

6. The Heavy and Medium T.M. emplacements of 38th. Divisional Artillery at present covering front of 39th. Division and Ammunition will be handed over to 39th. Divisional Artillery on May 5th. D.T.M.O's concerned will arrange details.

7. On May 6th. 122nd. Brigade will hand over their Wagon Lines to 174th. Brigade and move back to WATOU, and take over Lines and Billets of 174th. Brigade R.F.A.

8. On completion of this relief the present Centre Group will become Right Group, commanded by Lieut. Colonel G.P.MacCLELLAN. D.S.O. consisting of :-

    "B"/119.   "A"/121.
    "D"/119. (4 guns.) "B"/121.
                      "C"/121.
                      "D"/121.

39th. Divisional Artillery will have a call on "C"/121 for enfilade fire.

9. ACKNOWLEDGE.

C Geldard
Major R.A.
Brigade Major 38th. Divisional Artillery.

Issued at 9 a.m.
May 2nd. 1917.
Copies to:-
38th. Div. "G".
38th. Div. "Q".   R.A. Signal Officer   38th. Divl. Train.
122nd. Brigade (5).   Signals.   R.A. VIII Corps.
119th. Brigade (1).   C.R.E.   R.A. 39th. Division.
121st. Brigade (2).   A.D.M.S.
D.A.C.   (2).   A.D.V.S.
D.T.M.O.   (2).   S.S.O.

SECRET

Appendix "A".

Date	Unit.	Position.	Relieved by.	Moves to.	Remarks.
Night 4/5th.May	1 Section "B"/122.	B.29.a. 0. 0.	1 Section 18-pdr.Bty.174th.Bde.	Wagon Lines.	The gun teams and Limbers of Batteries 39th.Div.Arty. will have to double up for these nights in the 122nd.Bde.Wagon Lines.
	2 Sections "C"/122.	C.19.c.85.20 (2) C.26.d. 6. 4.(2)	2 Sections 18-pdr.Btys.174th.Bde.	—do—	
	2 Sections "D"/122.	C.25.d. 5. 2.(2) B.29.c. 7. 9.(2)	2 Sections "D"/174 Brigade.	—do—	
	1 Section "C"/121.	I. 7.a. 8. 9.	1 Section 18-pdr.Bty.174th.Bde.	Relieve 1 Sect "A"/122 at PARROY.	
	1 Section "A"/122.	PARROY.	1 Section "C"/121.	Wagon Lines.	
May 7th	B.A.C. *(handwritten)* No 2 Sect 3t Bde	A.21.a. 8. 7. *(handwritten A.21.a.8.3.)*	1 Section 39th.D.A.C.	HERZEELE D.2.c.5.8.	To be clear of present location before 12 noon – March via WATOU-HOUTKERQUE.
Night 5/6th.May	2 Sections "B"/122.	B.29.a. 0. 0.	2 Sections 18-pdr.Bty.174th.Bde.	Wagon Lines.	
	1 Section "C"/122. 1 Sec."D"/122.	C.19.c.85.20. C.25.d. 5. 2.	1 Section 18-pdr.Bty.174th.Bde. 1 Section "D"/174th.Bde.	—do— —do—	
	2 Sections "C"/121.	I. 7.a. 8. 9.	2 Sections 18-pdr.Bty.174th.Bde.	Relieves 2 Secs "A"/122 at PARROY.	
	2 Sections "A"/122.	PARROY.	2 Sections "C"/121 Brigade.	Wagon Lines.	
	H.Q. 122nd. Bde. R.F.A.	REIGERSBURG.	H.Q.174th.Brigade R.F.A.	Wagon Lines.	

SECRET.
Appendix "A". Sheet 2.

Date.	Unit.	Position.	Relieved by.	Moves to	Remarks.
May 6th.	H.Q.122nd. Brigade R.F.A. "A"/122. "B"/122. "C"/122. "D"/122.	Wagon Lines.	174th.Brigade.	WATOU.	To be clear of present Wagon Lines by 10 a.m. Route Via.L.4.b.9.2.

ADMINISTRATIVE INSTRUCTIONS TO ACCOMPANY R.A. ORDER

NO. 62. DATED 2nd MAY. 1917.

1. ~~On 5th May 1917 the 119th (Army) R.F.A.C. move into billets at HERZEELE (....) handing over their present Wagon Lines to a Section 39th D.A.C.~~ *Cancelled*

2. On 6th May 1917 the 122nd Bde. R.F.A. will move into billets at WATOU as follows:-
   A.122 at K5.a.6.5.   Sheet 27
   B.122 at K4.d.9.4.   "
   C.122 at K5.c.3.8.   "
   D.122 at K5.c.3.5.   "
   handing over their present Wagon Lines to 174th Bde R.F.A. (39th Division)

3. Lists of all Trench or Area Stores handed over to and taken over from 39th Division must be forwarded to this Office by noon 7th May 1917.

4. Ammunition at Gun Positions of C/121 Bde. B/122 Bde, C/122 Bde and D/122 Bde will be handed over to incoming units of 39th Division at 12. noon on 5th May 1917. Amounts handed over to be reported to Right Group (REIGERSBURGH) by 12.30 p.m.
   C/121 Bde will take over Ammunition at Gun Position from A/122 Bde at 12. noon 5th May 1917. Handing and taking over, reports to be sent to Right and Centre Groups by 12.30. p.m.
   Right and Centre Groups will report all transfers of Ammunition to R.A. Head Quarters by 2. p.m. 5th May 1917.

5. Echelons will move back to Reserve Area with full establishment of Ammunition and as far as possible with correct proportions:- ie. for 18. Pdr. Ammuntion 75% Shrapnel., 25% H.E.

6. The 38th D.A.C. will arrange to ~~move~~ *issue* the necessary Ammunition on 3rd. May 1917.

7. *No 2 Res. 38 DAC* ~~The 119th (Army) R.F.A.C.~~ during their stay in Reserve Area will be rationed by means of Light Railway from PROVEN in accordance with C.R.O. 1096 dated 25-4-17.

8. A Section of the Headquarter Coy. Divisional Train will move with the 122nd Bde to WATOU.
   Billets for this Detachment must be arranged by B.H. Quarters.
   Supplies on the 6th and subsequent dates will be picked up at PESELHOEK in the usual manner and delivered to WATOU.
   Horses for Baggage Wagons will arrive at Wagon Lines on the morning of the 6th. The loaded Wagons will march as a Train Column under A.S.C. arrangements, accompained by a Baggage Guard in each case
   On arrival at WATOU the wagons will be kept in Wagon Lines for Battery use and horses will return to the Train Detachment.

9. Advance parties should be sent by ~~119th Bde and~~ 122nd Bde Batteries to take over new Billets and Area Stores on 4th and 5th May respectively. *An advance party should be sent on 6th May by No 2 Res. 38 DAC to take over new Billets and Area Stores.*

10. A rear party will remain behind to hand over at each Wagon Line, and will not leave until a signed certificate is obtained from incoming unit that the billets and lines have been cleaned up to their satisfaction.
    These certificates to be forwarded to R.A. Headquarters as soon as relief is completed.

(2.)

11. An Officer from each unit must remain behind in accordance with billeting rules to receive, and, if possible, settle all claims etc., before leaving.

12. On 5th May 1917. the 122nd Bde will return to D.A.C. all G.S. Wagons received on loan and obtain receipts for same, showing the condition they are in.
Receipts to be forwarded to R. A. Headquarters.

13. Amended Bathing arrangements for Divisional Artillery and ~~/115th (Army) Bde~~ in consequence of above moves are being made and will be issued later.

// No 2 Ant. 38 DAC

14. Medical Arrangements.
M.O. 121st Bde will go to TROISTOURS and look at the Right Group.
M.O. from a Field Ambulance will look after all Wagon Lines 38th Division, Artillery.
M.O. from WORMHOUDT will look after ~~illegible~~ at HERZEELE.

No 2 Ant. 38 DAC

H R Graystone
Captain. R.A.
Staff Captain. R. A. 38th Division.

2-5-1917.

SECRET.

Amendment to 38th Divisional Artillery Operation Order

No. 62.

Para. 5.   Delete "119th B.A.C. will hand etc."-----------------
           "HERZEELE".
             and substitute
           "No. 2 Section 38th D.A.C. will be relieved by No. 1
           Section 39th D.A.C. on May 7th and move back to
           HERZEELE."

Appendix 'A'.   May 5th. to be amended accordingly.

                                              [signed]
                                              Major R.A.
5/5/17.   Brigade Major, 38th Divisional Artillery.

Copies to all recipients of O.O. 62.

D.A.C.

AMENDENMENT TO ADMINISTRATIVE INSTRUCTIONS TO ACCOMPANY R.A. ORDER No 62. dated 2nd MAY. 1917.

Cancel para 1. and substitute the following.

On 7th May 1917 No 2. Section 38th. D.A.C. will move into billets at HERZEELE (D.2.c.5.8,) handing over their present Wagon Lines to a Section 39th. D.A.C.

They should be clear of their present location before 10-30 a.m. and march Via WATOU- HOUTKERQUE.

Para 7. Line 1. For 119th (Army) B.A.C. read No. 2. Section 38th. D.A.C.

Para 9. An advance party should be sent on 6th May, by No. 2. Section D.A.C. to take over new Billets and Area Stores.

Para. 13. Line 2. For 119th (Army) Bde read No. 2. Section 38th. D.A.C.

Para 14. Last Line. For 119th B.A.C. read 38th. D.A.C.

5-5-1917.

Captain. R.A.
Staff Captain. R.A. 38th Division.

WAR DIARY
or
INTELLIGENCE SUMMARY

Army Form C. 2118

38th D.A.C. (W.A.C.)

Vol 19

Place	Date	Hour	Summary of Events and Information	Remarks and references to Appendices
DESELAGER	3/7		Lieut. J.D. ROBERTSON despatched to D/121	
COPPERNOLLE	6/7/17	6 a.m.	On 6/6/17 shells (15 cm. apparently fired from H.V. gun) commenced to fall close to Billets of No 3 Section. Shells continued to fall at intervals of about 20 minutes, but none fell on the camp til about 6.30 a.m. when a shell struck the farm house where Sergts Mess was occupying billets. The horses of No 3 Section were moved out to a flank, as 9 a.m. it was considered safe for them to return to their lines.	
		10.15 a.m.	Shelling recommenced and orders were given for horses of Headquarters, No 1 and No 3 Sections to be harnessed up and the men to return in direction to the east. The shell of the morning falling on No 1 Section damaged one horse killed and four others wounded. Two men of No 1 Section, one horse killed and four others wounded. Headquarters and No 3 Section got away without casualties. The lines of No 2 Section were shelled at about 12.45 p.m. this Section moved out at once. No casualties to men, three horses killed and seven wounded and a quantity of harness destroyed.	

Army Form C. 2118

WAR DIARY
or
INTELLIGENCE SUMMARY

38th D.A.C. (W Arc)

(Erase heading not required.)

Instructions regarding War Diaries and Intelligence Summaries are contained in F.S. Regs., Part II. and the Staff Manual respectively. Title Pages will be prepared in manuscript.

Place	Date	Hour	Summary of Events and Information	Remarks and references to Appendices
COPPERNOLLE	6/7/17		Some movement of the artillery, which was evidently intended for the new railway, which have been constructed near the camp at PESELHOEK. The two DAC two men spare to gun spare (M.10.d.7.7 sheet 29 BELGIUM).	AW
do	17/7		Lieut. F.R. SMITH joined from Base.	Ado
do	26/7		Lieut. J.C. PORTER joined from Cavalry Division. Capt W.M. MATHESON posted to B/111 Brigade. Lieut. T. HORLINGTON attached to 38th R.A.M.Q. The Camp was shelled last night and this morning 15 cm H.V. Gun. Shells commenced to fall in the Camp at 9.15 P.M. 25/9/17 and the horses were taken out at once. The rafters were spent at an old location at PESELHOEK. Shelling continued at intervals until about 4 am today. Casualties seven men wounded (one seriously), 24 horses killed and 20 wounded. 14 of the wounded horses had to be destroyed. All rations returned late as about 4 am today.	AW
do	27/7		I was seriously recommended 3 deputy warrant warrant of work, & made thirteen while obtaining ammunition to Gun Position Commander. Major G.T. GREGOR [signed] Lieut. C.S. WOODS — do —	AW 122 Brigade

1875 Wt. W593/826 1,000,000 4/15 J.B.C. & A. A.D.S.S./Forms/C. 2118.

Army Form C. 2118

WAR DIARY
or
INTELLIGENCE SUMMARY 15th Div. (W.A.C.)
(Erase heading not required.)

Instructions regarding War Diaries and Intelligence Summaries are contained in F.S. Regs., Part II. and the Staff Manual respectively. Title Pages will be prepared in manuscript.

Place	Date	Hour	Summary of Events and Information	Remarks and references to Appendices
OPPERDINGE	25.11		Capt. C.W.E. ALLEN posted as 19th Corp Heavy Artillery on Staff Captain	
do	27th		I am this afternoon visited billets delivery ammunition to guns batteries	
do	29th		Visited S.D. Echelons further from Dépôt.	

D. O'Reilly Lt. R. Fus.
for the G.O.C. 15 D. H. A.
16.

WAR DIARY
or
INTELLIGENCE SUMMARY

(Erase heading not required.)

Army Form C. 2118

38th D.A.C. (M.A.C.) Vol 2

Place	Date	Hour	Summary of Events and Information	Remarks and references to Appendices
Coppernolle	1/7		LIEUT. P.R. DANGERFIELD appointed Acting Adjutant vice Capt. C.W.E. ALLEN to XIX Corps Heavy Artillery. CAPT. J. PLUMMER was evacuated to England sick, and struck off the strength of this Unit with effect from 29th June 1917.	P.D.
"	10/7		At 5.45 p.m. the Camp was shelled by the enemy and LIEUT. R.G. HITCHINGS was killed by the explosion of a high velocity shell falling in the Officers Quarters near his tent.	P.D.
"	13/7		At 4.30 a.m. three enemy shells in No 2 Section severely wounding four drivers who were asleep in bed. In consequence of the constant shelling of the Camp, Trenches + Dug outs were made for the protection of the men.	P.D.
"	17/7		On this date the Camp was again shelled, eight animals being killed and fourteen wounded, 1 man was wounded and evacuated to Hospital.	P.D.
"	19/7		2/LIEUT. J.C. PORTER previously attached to this Unit, was posted to No 2 Section from Base Depot.	P.D.
"	20/7		At 2.30 p.m. the enemy shelled the road near our Dumps. One shell struck a lorry of one Dump and set alight the Camouflage Covering. The flames were soon extinguished by men of the Unit. The only damage done was the loss of a few Hessian Charges + Shells, also a quantity of camouflage.	P.D.

Army Form C. 2118

WAR DIARY
or
INTELLIGENCE SUMMARY

(Erase heading not required.)

38th D.A.C. (W.A.C.)

Instructions regarding War Diaries and Intelligence Summaries are contained in F.S. Regs., Part II. and the Staff Manual respectively. Title Pages will be prepared in manuscript.

Place	Date	Hour	Summary of Events and Information	Remarks and references to Appendices
COPPERNOLLE	21/7		2/Lieut. C.G. SPILLER joined from 72nd Army Field Artillery Brigade and posted to No 3 Sectn.	PS/1
	26/7		2nd/Lieut. R.G. Hitchings, to be actg Captain whilst comdg a Section 38th D.A.C. under date 21st June 1917. (Lieut R.G. Hitchings killed 10/7). List 1444 "Appointments, Commissions to."	PS/2
			14th July 1917.	
	27/7		No 1907 Driver T.G. Diggle, Headquarters D.A.C, awarded Military Medal by Corps Commander	PS/3
	31/7	9 a.m.	The Column formed advanced Dumps at G.23.b.2.8 (Sheet 28) portions of No 1 + 2 Sections were composed of 9ft Wagons being relieved for this purpose.	PS/4
	31/7	2 p.m.	All horses withdrawn from Forward Dumps, Lieutenant LEFF, Corps Ammunition Park Commander took over the Command of Lieut. Wagons	PS/5
			Supply of Ammunition to this Dump which did no was under the Command of Lieut. T. Hayes-Shear.	PS/6
			2/Lieut George Ernest Cashmore joined from Base. During the night 31/1/Augt 180 new + horses supplied the guns with ammunition by packs.	PS/7

Wm Hayes [signature]
Comdg. 36 DAC
3/1/17

1875 Wt. W593/826 1,000,000 4/15 J.B.C. & A. A.D.S.S./Forms/C. 2118.

Army Form C. 2118

WAR DIARY
or
INTELLIGENCE SUMMARY
(Erase heading not required.)

38th D.A.C. (M.T.O) Vol 21

Place	Date	Hour	Summary of Events and Information	Remarks and references to Appendices
COPPERNOLLE	1/8/17		2/Lieut. T. Hayes-Sheen promoted Acting Captain, with effect from 19th June 1917, whilst commanding a section of 38th D.A.C.	P.B.
-"-	5/8/17		T/Lieut. P.R. DANGERFIELD appointed Adjutant 38th D.A.C. with effect from 1st July 1917.	P.B.
-"-	6/8/17		2/Lieut. J.B.Y. CLEMENTS rejoined from Corps Ammunition Park.	P.B.
-"-	11/8/17		Three men Killed and one man wounded whilst delivering ammunition to the Guns.	P.B.
-"-	12/8/17		2/Lieut. G.E. CASHMORE posted to 122nd Brigade R.F.A.	P.B.
-"-	13/8/17		Three men Killed whilst delivering ammunition to the guns.	P.B.
-"-	21/8/17		2/Lieut. J. BEWLEY (Jr.) joined from Base.	P.B.
-"-	22/8/17		One man Killed whilst delivering ammunition to the guns.	P.B.
-"-	6/8/17		2/Lieut. J. BEWLEY posted to 122nd Brigade R.F.A.	P.B.
-"-	26/8/17		2/Lieut. F.R. SNALAM joined from Base.	P.B.
			Three men awarded the Military Medal by Corps Commander.	P.B.
			One man awarded the Military Medal by Corps Commander.	P.B.

Army Form C. 2118

WAR DIARY
INTELLIGENCE SUMMARY
(Erase heading not required.)

Instructions regarding War Diaries and Intelligence Summaries are contained in F.S. Regs., Part II. and the Staff Manual respectively. Title Pages will be prepared in manuscript.

Place	Date	Hour	Summary of Events and Information	Remarks and references to Appendices
COPPERNOLLE	28/8	8.20 pm	Bletchley Dump shelled by enemy and quantity of ammunition destroyed by Dump catching on fire — Fire lasted until 4 am. 29th Augt 1917	

M. Maynard
Lt. Col. R.G.A.
Comdg. 38' D.A.C.

1/9/17

1875 Wt. W593/826 1,000,000 4/15 J.B.C. & A. A.D.S.S./Forms/C. 2118.

Army Form C. 2118

WAR DIARY
INTELLIGENCE SUMMARY

(Erase heading not required.)

38th D.A.C. (VVAC) Vol 22

Place	Date	Hour	Summary of Events and Information	Remarks and references to Appendices
COPPERNOLLE	1/9/17		The Column re-organized with effect from this date in accordance with low Establishment Part VII A. No 642. The personnel and horses surplus to establishment on reorganization were posted to Brigades of the 38th Divisional Artillery and 141 men of the British West Indies Reg't were attached to this Unit for work on Ammunition Dumps. These men remained with the 20th Divisional Ammunition Column on relief.	
-"-	5/9/17		No 722, Cpl. W. QUICK, and No 404, Gr. W.T. ROGERS awarded MILITARY MEDAL for gallantry in connection with the fire at Bletchley Ammunition Dump on the 28th Aug't 1917.	
-"-	8/9/17		7/Lieut. P.R. DANGERFIELD promoted Acting Captain whilst holding the appointment as Adjutant, dated 3rd August 1917.	
-"-	10/9/17		2/Lieut. R.W. DOBSON awarded MILITARY CROSS for gallantry at Bletchley Dump fire 28th Aug't 1917. F. HORLINGTON posted to D/122 Brigade.	
-"-	11/9/17	4:30 p.m.	At this hour the Camp was shelled — Two enemy shells fell in No 1 Section horse lines killing two men and four horses.	
-"-	14/9/17		LIEUT. J.J. MUSKETT joined from Base and posted to No 3 Section. CAPT. T. MILLER Junior from C/122 and assumes command of H.Q.T. Section.	
-"-	15/9/17	4:30 a.m.	At this hour No 2 Section lines were shelled, two enemy shells falling in horse lines killing no animals.	
-"-	-"-	8.30 a.m.	The D.A.C. marched from COPPERNOLLE to STEENVOORDE.	
STEENVOORDE	16/9/17	8.45 a.m.	The Column marched from STEENVOORDE to LA CUNEWELE.	
LACUNEWELE	17/9/17	9.30 a.m.	The Column marched from LA CUNEWELE area to STEENBECQUE.	
STEENBECQUE	19/9/17		LIEUT. J.J. MUSKETT posted to 121 Brigade.	

Army Form C. 2118

WAR DIARY
INTELLIGENCE SUMMARY
(Erase heading not required.)

38th D.A.C. (M.A.C)

Place	Date	Hour	Summary of Events and Information	Remarks and references to Appendices
STEENBECQUE	19/2/17		The Column moved from STEENBECQUE to NEUF BERQUIN.	P/I
-"-	21/2/17		LIEUT. J.W.AIRD finds from Ammunition Column Cavalry Division.	P/I
			The Column moved from NEUF BERQUIN to ESTAIRES and took over Wagon Lines and Billets from 57th D.A.C. also Dumps and Bomb Store.	P/I
ESTAIRES	24/2/17		2/LIEUT. R.M.DOBSON promoted LIEUT. with effect from 1/2.	P/I
-"-			2/LIEUT. J.C.PORTER posted to 121 Brigade	P/I
-"-	26/2/17		2/LIEUT. J.B.V.CLEMENTS posted to 122 Brigade	P/I
-"-	29/2/17		LIEUT. T.D.WILLIAMS found unfit for General Service by Medical Board and struck off the strength of the Column accordingly	P/I

30/2/17

Capt. for Lt. Col. R.F.A.
Commdg. 38/Div. Ammunition Column.

Army Form C. 2118

WAR DIARY
INTELLIGENCE SUMMARY
(Erase heading not required.)

38th D.A.C. (N.Z.)

Vol 23

Place	Date	Hour	Summary of Events and Information	Remarks and references to Appendices
ESTAIRES	26/7/17		Temp. Lieut. A.W. WILLIAMS promoted Acting Captain whilst commanding a Section of D.A.C., with effect from 30.6.17.	PP./p/
			2/Lieut. F.R. SMITH posted to 122nd Brigade R.F.A.	PP./p/
	28/7/17		2/Lieut. E.R. STANTON, (T.F.) joined from Base.	PP./p/

E Hayward
Lt. Col. RFA
Comdg. 38th D.A.C.

1/11/17

WAR DIARY

INTELLIGENCE SUMMARY

Army Form C. 2118

38D Am Col
Vol 24

Place	Date	Hour	Summary of Events and Information	Remarks and references to Appendices
ESTAIRES	11/11/17		2/Lieut. J.D. ROBERTSON granted extension by Medical Board whilst on leave in England and struck off strength this unit with effect from 11th Novr 1917.	
"			2/Lieut. E.R. STANTON posted to D/122 Brigade	

M.D. Hayward Lt Col RFA
Comdg 38th D.A.C.
1/12/17

Army Form C. 2118

WAR DIARY
or
INTELLIGENCE SUMMARY
(Erase heading not required.)

38th D.A.C. (M.A.C.)   W 25

Instructions regarding War Diaries and Intelligence Summaries are contained in F.S. Regs., Part II. and the Staff Manual respectively. Title Pages will be prepared in manuscript.

Place	Date	Hour	Summary of Events and Information	Remarks and references to Appendices
ESTAIRES	15/2/17		Lieut. Col. C.W. HAYWARD and Lieut (a/Capt) P.R. DANGERFIELD mentioned in Dispatches (London Gazette Dec 14/17)	P.A.
	27/2/17		2/Lieut F. ARBUCKLE joined from Base.	P.A.
	28/2/17		-"- W.E. AUSTIN " " "	P.A.
	-"-		-"- T. GREENWOOD " " "	P.A.
	29/2/17		-"- H.E.B. WILLIAMS " " "	P.A.

E.W. Hayward Lt. Col. R.F.A.
Comdg. 38 D.A.C.

1/3/18.

WAR DIARY or **INTELLIGENCE SUMMARY**

Army Form C. 2118

38 D Am Col

Vol 26

Place	Date	Hour	Summary of Events and Information	Remarks and references to Appendices
ESTAIRES	1/8		Lieut Col G.W. HAYWARD awarded D.S.O.	App.
	9/8		2/Lieut F. ARBUCKLE posted to Y332 Bgd. R.F.A.	App.
	10/8		2/Lieut T. GREENWOOD posted to 57th Div: Arty.	App.
			— " — H.E.B. WILLIAMS "	App.
	17/8		The Column moved from ESTAIRES to HAVERSKERQUE area taking over billets	App.
			Lines re. from 12th D.A.C.	App.
	26/8		Lieut. F.L. HYBART joined from 121 Bgd. R.F.A.	App.

W Seymour
Lt Col R.F.A.
Comdg. 38 D.A.C.
31-1-16

Army Form C. 2118

WAR DIARY
INTELLIGENCE SUMMARY
(Erase heading not required.)

38½ D.A.C. (V.A.C.)

9/M/27

Place	Date	Hour	Summary of Events and Information	Remarks and references to Appendices
HAVERSKERQUE	6/2/18		2/Lieut. S.H.SIDDALLS joined on posting from Base.	B/--
-"-	15/2/18		142 Indian Personnel joined the Column.	B/--
-"-	17/2/18		The Column moved from HAVERSKERQUE area to STEENWERCKE area taking over Billets, Lines, etc. from 57½ D.A.C.	B/--

[signed] Capt. J. Ellrott
Comdg. 38 DAC

1/3/16

WAR DIARY
or
INTELLIGENCE SUMMARY

Army Form C. 2118

38 D Amm Col

Vol 28

Place	Date	Hour	Summary of Events and Information	Remarks and references to Appendices
STEENWERK	1/3/18		2/Lt. H. SMITH joined from Base.	
" —	19/3/18		2/Lt. H. SMITH posted to 122 Brigade R.F.A.	
" —	22/3/18		Lieut W.T. GORNALL posted to ENGLAND under W.O. instructions.	
" —	25/3/18		2/Lt. D.C. REES posted to T.M.B.	
" —	28/3/18		" " H.C. MOORE " " — " —	
" —	29/3/18		" " C.N. FAIRBURN attached to "B" A.A. Bty.	
" —	30/3/18		Lieut F.L. HYBART posted to 59th Divl. Arty.	
" —	30/3/18		No 3 (S.A.A.) Section moved from STEENWERCK area to HAVERSKERQUE area under command of Lieut J.W. AIRD.	

31/3/16.

Lt Colonel
Comdg 38 D.A.C.

V.Corps.
Third Army.

WAR DIARY

38th DIVISIONAL AMMUNITION COLUMN.

A P R I L

1 9 1 8

WAR DIARY
INTELLIGENCE SUMMARY

38th D.A.C. (Y.T.A.C.)

Army Form C. 2118

(Erase heading not required.)

Place	Date	Hour	Summary of Events and Information	Remarks and references to Appendices
STEENWERK	7/78	9.45 am	Left Le Kilem, STEENWERK, for HAVERSKERQUE area (New S.A.P. Schlo with Div. H.Q.)	P/
HAVERSKERQUE	8/78	2 pm	Attached to 34th Div. Artillery and ordered to NEUF BERQUIN arriving there at 4.30 pm. Formed Ammunition Dump at DOULIEU Church - supplies ammunition to the Brigades of 34th Artillery - 152 Brigade and 160 Brigade - whilst same moved to rear of Dump in the evening, when, owing to enemy shell fire, Dump was abandoned.	P/
NEUF BERQUIN	8/78	midnight	Moved to La MOTTE, Rue de Bois, and supplies ammunition to guns from Army Dump at VIEUX BERQUIN.	P/
LA MOTTE	11/78	6 pm	Moves to field at Gd Sec Bois.	P/
Gd SEC BOIS	12/78	9 am	Moves to field near BORRE.	P/
BORRE		1 pm	Left BORRE for MORBECQUE where 34th French Mortars under command of Capt. Renie M.C. joined us for duty. French Mortar personnel assisted us with our Dumps which were formed at Le GRAND HAZARD and near MORBECQUE CHATEAU for supply of Ammunition.	P/
MORBECQUE	20/78	2 pm	Moves from vicinity of MORBECQUE to neighbourhood of road at BOIS des HUIT RUES but continues supply Dumps as above.	P/
BOIS des HUIT RUES	21/78	3 pm	2/Lt B.W.H. MOSS, R.F.A. joined from 38th Div. Arty and attached pending orders.	P/
	24/78	9 am	A/Capt B.W.H. MOSS, R.F.A. proceeded to England with machine-gun officer, in writing, on arrival.	P/

R.H. Stafford Lt Col
Artillery 38 D.A.C.

Army Form C. 2118

WAR DIARY

INTELLIGENCE SUMMARY   38th D.A.C. (N.A.C.)

(Erase heading not required.)

Vol 30

Place	Date	Hour	Summary of Events and Information	Remarks and references to Appendices
MORBECQUE (Bois des Huit Rues)	7/5/18	8 a.m.	H.Q. & No.1 Section left for ST JAN TER BIEZEN area to rejoin 38th Divl. Artly, and came under orders 33rd Artillery taking over Ammunition Dump.	R.P.
— " —	8/5/18	— " —	No 2 Section left for ST JAN TER BIEZEN area to rejoin H.Q. No1 Section with 38th Divl. Artillery.	R.P.
ST JAN ter BIEZEN	13/5/18		2/Lieut. S.H. SIDDALS posted to "J" Battery A.R.	R.P.
	15/5/18	10·30 a.m.	H.Q. No1 & 2 Sections moved from ST JAN ter BIEZEN area to PROVEN district	R.P.
	18/5/18		The Column (less S.A.A. Sectn) entrained from PROVEN area, to join the Division, in DOULLENS area and went into Billets at GEZAINCOURT.	R.P.
GEZAINCOURT.	21/5/18		2/Lieut. H.G. FRANCE joined from D/121 Bgde.	R.P.
	23/5/18		A/Capt. J.H. RIMMER posted to Command S.A.A. Sectn from D/121 (R.A. 9.3879/6/3).	R.P.
			Lieut. J.W. AIRD relinquishes temporary command of S.A.A. on posting of Capt. RIMMER	R.P.
			A/Capt. T. HAYES-SHEEN to revert to LIEUTENANT on ceasing to command No 3 Sectn on from 29th March 1918.	R.P.
	27/5/18		LIEUT. W.J. ADKINS joined from Base.	R.P.
			2/LIEUT. A.H. BERNARD " " " "	R.P.
			2/LIEUT. W.J. DODD " " " "	R.P.
	31/5/18	11 a.m.	The Column (less S.A.A.) marches to RAINCHEVAL area.	R.P.

1/6/18

R.O. Shepherd Jr. Col. R.F.A.
Commdg. 38 D.A.C.

Army Form C. 2118

WAR DIARY
or
INTELLIGENCE SUMMARY
(Erase heading not required.)

38th D.A.C. (H.Q.)   June 1918

Place	Date	Hour	Summary of Events and Information	Remarks and references to Appendices
RAINCHEVAL	10/6/18		Headquarters DAC moved to LILLEVILLERS area and took over A.R.P. at HARPONVILLE.	R.
	11/6/18	10 a.m.	9 18 pdr and 6 4.5 Howitzer L.E.S. wagons moved to HARPONVILLE and Advanced Section for 124 Brigade.	R.
	14/6/18	10 a.m.	LIEUT. M.C.DEACON posted from 78th Brigade and remains attached II Corps. 9 18 pdr and 6 4.5 Howitzer wagons moved to HARPONVILLE as an Advanced Section for 122 Brigade.	R. R.
	23/6/18		Established as a Divisional Ammunition Column returned by 36 Division and 72 Light Draught Animals (vide II Corps YB/8053 of 20.6.18)	R.
	24/6/18		LIEUT. A.S. BLYTH joined from Base and posted to No 3 Section.	R.
	27/6/18		LIEUT. J.W.BAIRD posted to 122 Brigade as Horsemaster.	R.

M.D.Heyworth
Lt. Col.
Comdg. 38 D.A.C.

1/7/18

Army Form C. 2118

WAR DIARY
INTELLIGENCE SUMMARY
(Erase heading not required.)

38th D.A.C. (R.F.A.) W.A. Corps

WD 32

Place	Date	Hour	Summary of Events and Information	Remarks and references to Appendices
RAINCHEVAL	6/7/18		Lieut. M.G. DEACON to 35th D.A.	R.
"	7/7/18		Lieut. F.R. SMITH joined from Base.	R.
"	17/7/18		A.R.P. at HARPONVILLE handed over to 17th D.A.C.	R.
"	12/7/18		Lieut. A. FITTES posted from 12th D.A.C. and remains attached V Corps.	R.
"	27/7/18		Lieut. T. HAYES-SHEEN struck off strength.	R.
"	29/7/18	10 am	Advanced wagon lines of Nos 1 + 2 Sections rejoined Rear Lines at RAINCHEVAL.	R.

1/8/18

[signature]
Lt. Col. R.F.A.
Commanding 38th D.A.C.

WAR DIARY
or
INTELLIGENCE SUMMARY

(Erase heading not required.)

Army Form C. 2118

38th D.A.C. (R.F.A.)

Vol 33

Place	Date	Hour	Summary of Events and Information	Remarks and references to Appendices
RAINCHEVAL	1/8/18		Lieut T. HAYES-SHEEN rejoined from Hospital	
"	1/8/18		Lieut G.D. THOMAS joined from 122 Bde R.F.A and posted to No 1. Section	
"	6/8/18		Lieut A. ST. CLAIR BLYTHE posted to 122 Bgd R.F.A.	
"	6/8/18		A.R.P. at HARPONVILLE taken over from 17th D.A.C.	
"	9/8/18		Salvage Dump established at HEDAUVILLE for ammunition.	
"	15/8/18		Nos 1 + 2 Sections moved to HARPONVILLE	
"	16/8/18		Lieut S.G. BURROWS of I.A.R. joined and posted to No 3 Section.	
"	19/8/18		Lieut W.G. AUSTEN attached to "N" Bty A.A.	
"	23/8/18		Lieut F.A. ARNOLD joined from Base and posted to No 3 Section	
"	24/8/18		No 3 Section detached & came under orders of 38th Div "Q"	
"	24/8/18		38th Div. T.M. attached to 38th D.A.C.	
HEDAUVILLE	24/8/18		O.H.Q. + No 1 + 2 Sections moved to HEDAUVILLE	
ALBERT	25/8/18		A.R.P. established at BOUZINCOURT and Nos 1+2 Sections moved to vicinity of dump. Later in the day A.R.P established in USNA VALLEY in front of ALBERT and H.Q. + No 1 + 2 Sections moved there in the evening.	
CONTAL-MAISON	27/8/18		A.R.P. established at CONTALMAISON. H.Q. + Nos 1 + 2 Sections moved to CONTALMAISON.	

Army Form C. 2118

WAR DIARY
or
INTELLIGENCE SUMMARY
(Erase heading not required.)

38th D.A.C. (R.F.A)

Place	Date	Hour	Summary of Events and Information	Remarks and references to Appendices
CONTAL-MAISON	28/8/16		A.R.P. established near POZIERES.	AWB
MAMETZ WOOD	29/8/16		A.R.P. established near LONGUEVAL. D.H.Q. & Nos 1 & 2 Sections moved to neighbourhood of MAMETZ WOOD.	AWB

Endkywood Lieut. Col.
Comdg 38th D.A.C.

1/9/16

WAR DIARY or INTELLIGENCE SUMMARY

Army Form C. 2118

38 D. Amm. Col. Vol 34

Place	Date	Hour	Summary of Events and Information	Remarks and references to Appendices
TRONES WOOD	2/9/18		A.R.P. established near DELVILLE WOOD. Hd.2rs & No 1 & 2 Sections moved to neighbourhood of TRONES WOOD.	
"	3/9/18		A.R.P. established near SAILLY SAILLISEL.	
LE SARS	7/9/18		A.R.P's handed over to 21st Div: Hd.2rs & No 1 & 2 Sections moved to neighbourhood of LE SARS and came under orders of 17th Div: Arty:	
BUS	10/9/18		Hd.2rs & No 1 & 2 Sections moved to neighbourhood of BUS.	
YTRES?	12/9/18		A.R.P's taken over from 17th D.A.C. at YTRES WOOD. Hd.2rs & No 1 & 2 Sections moved to neighbourhood of YTRES WOOD. T.M's came under orders of D.T.M.O.	
"	15/9/18	9.p.m	A bomb dropped by E.A. on Hd.2rs & No lines killing one Indian Dr. wounding the R.S.M. (died next day), the R.S.M. & 6 O.R. 2 horses killed or had to be destroyed.	
"	16/9/18		Temporary A.R.P's established near FINS and on FINS/METZ Rd.	
"	21/9/18	noon	A.R.P handed over to 17th Div.	
"	22/9/18		Lieut W.G. AUSTEN rejoined from "N" Bty A.A. F. ARNOLD struck off strength of 3rd Div Arty. & DAC. no. from 23/9/18. Auth. 32/KSH.	
"	26/9/18	noon	Came under orders of 21st Div Arty. at noon.	
"	29/9/18		No 1 Section came under orders of 63rd Div: Arty.	
"	30/9/18	0.5.am	Awards of MILITARY MEDALS. 36613 Cpl. H. COLE (Bar to M.M.), S⁹⁴ A. RICHARDS W/1951 and W/14996 S⁹⁴ R. KERSHAW.	

Lt Colonel Commanding 38 DAC

WAR DIARY or INTELLIGENCE SUMMARY

Army Form C. 2118

Vol. 35

38th D.A.C. (R.F.A.)

Place	Date	Hour	Summary of Events and Information	Remarks and references to Appendices
VALLULART WOOD	1/10/18		Moved to DESSART WOOD and No 1 Sechi to SOREL-LE-GRAND.	B.
DESSART WOOD	5/10/18		Came under 38th D.A.lly. HQ, No 1 + 2 Sechi moved to where A.R.P. was established at CATALET VALLEY.	B.
CATALET VALLEY	6/10/18		HQ, 1 + 2 Sechi moved to OTTUS WOOD. A.R.P established at LA TERRIERE.	B.
OTTUS WOOD	8/10/18		HQ, 1 + 2 Sechi moved over CANAL de L'ESCAUT to neighbourhood HONNECOURT.	B.
HONNECOURT	9/10/18		Came under orders of 33rd Div. D.Ally and A.R.P. handed over to them.	B.
	10/10/18		HQ, 1 + 2 Sechi moved to MAINCOURT and later in the day to CLARY.	B.
CLARY	14/10/18		A.R.P. at TROISVILLES taken over from 33 Divn.	B.
	15/10/18		HQ, 1 + 2 Sechi move to neighbourhood of BERTRY.	B.
BERTRY	24/10/18		HQ, 1 + 2 Sechi moved to MONTAY.	B.
	18/10/18		Lt. FRANCE posted to 121st Bgde.	B.
	8/10/18		Lt. AUSTEN to England (Cauby 8/G.H.)	B.
	1/10/18		Lt. C.G. STILLER to England (Cauby 8/G.H.)	B.

M. Hoyland Lt.Col. R.F.A.
Cmdg. 38th D.A.C.
1/11/18.

Army Form C. 2118

WAR DIARY
or
INTELLIGENCE SUMMARY

38th DAC (RFA)

(Erase heading not required.)

Vol. 36

Place	Date	Hour	Summary of Events and Information	Remarks and references to Appendices
MONTAY	5th/11	0700	H.Qrs, Nos 1 & 2 Sections moved to WAGONVILLE.	—
WAGONVILLE	6th/11	1400	The Column as above moved to Les GRANDE PATURES.	—
GRANDE PATURE	14th/11	0800	Moved to AULNOYE.	—
			2Lt. FRANCE rejoined from 121 Brigade.	—

1/12/18

M. Humphreys Lt. Col. RFA
Comdg. 38th DAC

Army Form C. 2118

WAR DIARY
or
INTELLIGENCE SUMMARY
(Erase heading not required.)

38th D.A.C. (RFA)

Vol 37

Instructions regarding War Diaries and Intelligence Summaries are contained in F. S. Regs, Part II. and the Staff Manual respectively. Title Pages will be prepared in manuscript.

Place	Date	Hour	Summary of Events and Information	Remarks and references to Appendices
AULNOYE	28/XI/18		The Column (Complete) moved to Montay, en route to Back area.	P.S.
MONTAY	29/XI/18		The Column moved to Masnières	P.S.
MASNIÈRES	30/XI/18		The Column moved to MANANCOURT.	P.S.
MANANCOURT	31/XI/18		The Column moved to ALBERT.	P.S.

Leyba??ful
Cpt RFA
adjt 38th DAC
for M.C. Cmdg

31/11/18.

Army Form C. 2118

WAR DIARY
or
INTELLIGENCE SUMMARY

38th D.A.C. (R.F.A.)

(Erase heading not required.)

Instructions regarding War Diaries and Intelligence Summaries are contained in F. S. Regs., Part II. and the Staff Manual respectively. Title Pages will be prepared in manuscript.

Place	Date	Hour	Summary of Events and Information	Remarks and references to Appendices
AILLY-SUR-SOMME	28/11/18		The Column (Complete) moved to Montay, en route to Back area.	P/
MONTAY	29/11/18		The Column moved to MOEUVRES	P/
MASNIÈRES	30/11/18		The Column moved to RIBANCOURT.	P/
RIBANCOURT	31/11/18		The Column moved to ALBERT.	P/

Ser.f. Bazalgette
Capt. R.F.A.
Adjt. 38th D.A.C.
for Lt. Col. Comdg

31/11/18

Army Form C. 2118

WAR DIARY
INTELLIGENCE SUMMARY
(Erase heading not required.)

38th D.A.C. (R.F.A.)

Instructions regarding War Diaries and Intelligence Summaries are contained in F.S. Regs., Part II. and the Staff Manual respectively. Title Pages will be prepared in manuscript.

Place	Date	Hour	Summary of Events and Information	Remarks and references to Appendices
ALBERT	1/1/19	0925	H.Q., 1 & 2 Sections moved into Billets at MONTIGNY, No 3 Sec. at BEHENCOURT.	P.J.
MONTIGNY	22/1/19		Capt. A. WYN WILLIAMS proceeded to U.K. for demobilization. – Lieut. W.J. ADKINS assumed command of No 2 Section vice Capt. A. WYN WILLIAMS.	P.J. B.
	24/1/19		2/Lt. P.B. WILLAN to U.K. for demobilization.	P.J. B.
	28/1/19		Capt. J.H. RIMMER to U.K. for demobilization. Lieut. G.P. THOMAS took over Command of No. 3 (How.) Section, vice Capt. J.H. RIMMER.	P.J. B.
			Capt. P.R. DANGERFIELD mentioned in Despatches. New Years Honours Gazette.	

Ino Hayward Lt Col
Comdg. 38 DAC
1/2/19

Army Form C. 2118

WAR DIARY
INTELLIGENCE SUMMARY
(Erase heading not required.)

38th D.A.C. (R.F.A.)

9/81 37

Place	Date	Hour	Summary of Events and Information	Remarks and references to Appendices
MONTIGNY	2/2/19		Lieut A. FITTES struck off strength 29-1-19. (Authy III Army A/c/50/3010, RA 38th Div 58/7110/6/3.	P/P
	6/2/19		" F.R. SNADEN to U.K. for demobilization.	P/P
			" H.H. MARSDEN to U.K. for demobilization	P/P
		12:00	H.R.H. The Prince of Wales inspected personnel of D.A.C. at x Rds Montigny/Rainneval	P/P
			2/Lieut H.G. FRANCE struck off strength (evacuated sick to U.K. 31.1.19)	P/P
	7/2/19		" R.W. WHINERAY to U.K. for demobilization.	P/P
	10/2/19		Personnel of Trench Mortar absorbed in D.A.C.	P/P
	21/2/19		B.Q.M.Sgt W.T. JONES, No3 Section, awarded Military Medal. (V Corps R. Order 2179)	P/P

Reg Campbell
Capt. R.F.A.
Comdg 38th D.A.C.
(Lt Col Coy sick in Hospital)

Army Form C. 2118

WAR DIARY
INTELLIGENCE SUMMARY
(Erase heading not required.)

38th D.A.C. (R.F.A.)

Place	Date	Hour	Summary of Events and Information	Remarks and references to Appendices
MONTIGNY.	6/3/19		Lieut. S.G. BURROW. I.A.R. to U.K. for demobilization 22.2.19.	P.R.
	10/3/19		" F.R. SMITH, R.F.A. to U.K. (sick) struck off strength 28.2.19.	P.R.
			Capt. W. HERBERTSON, R.A.M.C. to U.K. for demobilization.	P.R.
	15/3/19		Lieut (A/Capt) T. MILLER, R.F.A. posted to Home Establishment	P.R.
			Lieut. C.H. MOORE, posted to 122 Bgde R.F.A.	P.R.
	21/3/19		Rev. D.J. WATKINS-JONES, C.F. to 121 Bgde. R.F.A.	P.R.
			H.Q. 1 & 2 sections moved to GLISY.	P.R.
			No 3 section moved from BEHENCOURT to GLISY.	P.R.
			Took over Corps Vehicle Park.	P.R.
	22/3/19		Lieut W.J. ADKINS appointed A/Captain whilst Officer Comdg 38th D.A.C. } hat 228 Offs Commens to	P.R.
			" Capt Shannon "	

21/3/19

Reginald Buck
Capt. R.F.A.
Comdg 38th D.A.C.

Army Form C. 2118

WAR DIARY
or
INTELLIGENCE SUMMARY   38th D.A.C. (Ayr) R.F.A.
(Erase heading not required.)

Instructions regarding War Diaries and Intelligence Summaries are contained in F.S. Regs., Part II. and the Staff Manual respectively. Title Pages will be prepared in manuscript.

April 1919

Place	Date	Hour	Summary of Events and Information	Remarks and references to Appendices
Glasy	10th/19		Lieut G.P. TWIBILL joined from "D/122" Bde	P.J.
	14th/19		Lieut H. BODDITCH, R.E. to I Corps Concentration Camp. (Authority I Corps V.A. 642)	P.J.
	17th/19		Night 16/17 Stationery Box Stolen from Office. Enquiry held 18th/19 - Firing Parties attached Marks Co. or other known. Box contained Imprest Book A.F.W./R.F.A. 3197. Duplicate Acq Rolls Mch/Apl 1919. A.F.W. 3100 (Nos 286126-286150.) Field Cashier's Book. Current 1521 P. no no local corr in the Box when stolen.	P.J.
	18th/19		Lt. Col. G.W. Hayward, D.S.O. to England. (Authy 8/401.)	P.J.

1/5/19.

George Boughfield
Capt. R.F.A.
Comdg 38th D.A.C. (Ayr)

30th Divisional Ammunition Column
Re. J.A.
38 D.A.C.
R.J.A. May 1919.

WAR DIARY
or
INTELLIGENCE SUMMARY
(Erase heading not required.)

Army Form C. 2118

Place	Date	Hour	Summary of Events and Information	Remarks and references to Appendices
Etaing	1/5/19	—	Lieut O.S. Jones M.C. R.J.A. rejoined to S.R. and struck off strength with effect from 22.5.19	—
	9/5/19		Stationary Box station on night 16/17 April moved from Poeuk at Etaing 9/5/19	—
	21/5/19		Orders of 121 and 122 Brigades provided horse drafts to S.P. Headquarters, Motley and 150 stimulants O.R's herein at from 22.5/19	—
	26/5/19		Lieut J.P. Bolters R.J.A. proceeded to report to War Office	—
	31/5/19		Lieut J. H. Motley and 150 O.R's dispatched by train from Amiens to 2 W Army Ammunition camp Blerum	—

Strength left in
Country 35 O.R's own

R.A.

www.ingramcontent.com/pod-product-compliance
Lightning Source LLC
Chambersburg PA
CBHW081529160426
43191CB00011B/1716